Our Catholic Symbols

A RICH SPIRITUAL HERITAGE

OUR CATHOLIC SYMBOLS

A RICH SPIRITUAL HERITAGE

MICHAEL J. DALEY

TWENTY THIRD 23rd
PUBLICATIONS
www.23rdpublications.com

TWENTY-THIRD PUBLICATIONS
A Division of Bayard
One Montauk Avenue, Suite 200
New London, CT 06320
(860) 437-3012 or (800) 321-0411
www.23rdpublications.com

Cover images (left to right): DesignPics.com; iStockphoto.com/ Gianluca Fabrizio; Jupiterimages Corporation

ISBN 978-1-58595-753-8
Library of Congress Catalog Card Number: 2009926114
Printed in the U.S.A.

Contents

INTRODUCTION
Symbols: More than Meets the Eye 1

CHAPTER 1
Core Symbols of Catholicism. 4

CHAPTER 2
Symbols of a Church, Our Home of Faith . . . 19

CHAPTER 3
Symbolic Persons from Scripture. 33

CHAPTER 4
Saints as Symbolic Persons. 48

CHAPTER 5
Saints as Symbols of Virtue 63

CHAPTER 6
Symbols of the Christian Journey 79

CHAPTER 7
Symbols of the Mass. 97

INTRODUCTION

Symbols:
More than Meets the Eye

On walking into a Catholic church for the first time, many people are struck by how visually appealing it is. Their eyes are drawn to the stained glass windows, candles, holy water fonts, sculptures and statuary, Stations of the Cross, crucifix, tabernacle, altar, and lectern. One gets the sense that something is being said even though no words are spoken. Long before the printed words, the faith was taught through these "bibles in stone." Such is the power of symbols.

Unlike signs, which point to things in a rather straightforward fashion, symbols represent things more profound than they themselves are. Unfortunately, many Catholics do not know or are unaware of the Church's vast treasury of symbols. In the pages that follow the reader will be introduced to and given the opportunity to explore some of these symbols and the powerful realities they communicate to us.

One important reality is the Catholic principle of sacramentality—that the divine, the unnamed and unknowable mystery, is made visible and real to us in and through the

1

material. Bread, wine, water, physical gestures, art, and the like, can and do lead to the sacred. Or, in other words, there is more here than meets the eye. Indeed, symbols appeal to all our senses—sight, sound, taste, touch, and smell.

The *Catechism of the Catholic Church* conveys the insight that "In human life, signs and symbols occupy an important place. As a being at once body and spirit, man expresses and perceives spiritual realities through physical signs and symbols. As a social being, man needs signs and symbols to communicate with others, through language, gestures, and actions. The same holds true for his relationship with God" (#1146).

This is a very incarnational way of thinking and living. God became human in the person of Jesus of Nazareth. God also reveals God's self to us in the multiple symbols connected with our faith tradition. In fact, it could be said that symbols are the very language of faith. This book is but one humble attempt at expanding and appreciating our faith tradition.

As you'll discover reading the book, good symbols have a way of "repeating" themselves. On more than one occasion in the book, I'll return to the classic Christian symbols of Jesus, Spirit, Eucharist, Scripture, Fire, Water, and Community/Assembly. Each time, however, I'll be looking at the symbol in a related, but different way. I believe this is what all the great symbols open themselves up to—multiple meanings. As with life, when you change the perspective, new insights emerge. It is true with the symbols of faith as well.

As much as I would like to take all the credit for this project, this is simply not the case. My thanks go out to the editors I have worked with at Twenty-Third over the years—Gwen Costello, Alison Berger, Nick Wagner, Dan Connors, and Paul Pennick. Their acceptance of, support for, and improvement upon the work here is much appreciated. Finally, I wish to thank those closest to me for their constant patience and encouragement. This work would not be possible were it not for them—June, Cara, Brendan, and Nora.

CHAPTER 1

Core Symbols of Catholicism

JESUS: THE ULTIMATE SYMBOL OF GOD

In the course of a conversation about evolution, one of my students spoke of the "evolution" symbol that he'd seen on a neighbor's car. "It's a fish with legs." Bobby said. "What about the signs with just a fish on them?" remarked another. "What do they mean?"

In the ancient world, the fish was a staple of life. People needed it to live. In a similar way, Christians soon discovered that they needed their faith in Jesus to live as his followers. Using the Greek word for fish, *ichthys*, as an acronym, the early Christians were able to explain the substance of their faith simply and profoundly: "Jesus Christ, Son of God, Savior."

Jesus (Ieosus)

As is true in any family, when our daughter was born, her name rooted her in a particular family, during a particular time, in a particular place. It did the same for Jesus—he was son of Mary and, as tradition says, stepson of Joseph, who lived during the first century in a town called Nazareth.

Names can also define our role, our mission. Jesus'
name comes from the Hebrew name *Joshua*. It means "God
saves." That wasn't just a nice phrase; for Jesus it defined
and shaped his life. More important, it proclaimed him to
be a member of the human family (Matthew 1:21).

Christ (Christos)

Next I asked my class the question, "What does *Christ*
mean?" Andrew responded, "Isn't that Jesus' last name?"
Christ comes from the Greek, *Christos*, which comes from
the Hebrew word *messiah*. Whichever word you use, they
mean the same thing, "anointed one."

It refers to the long-awaited descendant of David, Israel's
legitimate ruler promised in Scripture. God was seen to be
at work in and through the anointed one. In Luke's Gospel,
Jesus referred to himself as being anointed (4:14–30).

Son of God (Theou Yios)

In most cases Scripture uses the title, "son of God," in a
metaphorical, or figurative, way. The Hebrew Scriptures
use it to refer to someone who has a special relationship
with God, usually the king (2 Samuel 7:14), or Israel itself
(Exodus 4:12; Hosea 11:1; Jeremiah 31:9, 20).

However, unlike most of these other examples, when we
call Jesus the "son of God" we mean it. Literally. We're not
saying he's *like* God; we're saying he *is* God, that he has a
divine nature.

Savior (Soter)

"Who's going to win the game this weekend?" I asked. In
unison the kids declared, "The Browns. It's always the other
team." What the Cincinnati Bengals need is a savior.

Since the sin of Adam, humanity was mired in a losing
streak. Our attempts at relationship with God were frus-

trated with selfish desires. In Jesus, we see the one person who can right the wrong. Jesus, through the example of his life on earth, shows us what it means to live freely and fully. He truly saves us.

TRINITY: A MYSTERY TO BE LIVED

Are you a mystery buff? Here's one neither Agatha Christie nor Sherlock Holmes can solve. Our Christian tradition speaks of God as triune, three persons—Father, Son, and Holy Spirit—each person God. How can that be? Distinct yet one? Different yet equal? When we try to "explain" the Trinity we trip over our explanations, and language fails us. We end by saying, "It's a mystery."

Thankfully, though, we're still left with the vocabulary of symbols. They powerfully communicate the central characteristics, so to speak, of the Trinity—the equality and diversity of the Father, Son, and Holy Spirit, their relationship to one another, and their community of love.

Nature Reveals the Trinity

A rich treasury of symbols for the Trinity comes from nature. I was reminded of this recently when I was bike riding with my family. Meandering alongside the bike path was a river. Tertullian, an early (160–220 AD) Christian teacher, used the image of a river to illustrate the mystery of the Trinity. The Father, like the source of the river, is the beginning. From the Father, the foundation of all life, flows the Son, just as the river waters pass through countless valleys and towns downstream. As it continues through the land, the river is used to irrigate the fields and provide water for drinking. Such is the power of the Holy Spirit to sustain and bring forth new life.

Building upon another image of Tertullian's (the sun), Saint Augustine (354–430 AD) suggested fire as a metaphor for the Trinity. The fire itself models the Father. The light penetrating the darkness of night symbolizes the Son. The warmth radiating from the logs represents the Holy Spirit. Another image Augustine used is based upon the First Letter of John: "God is love" (4:16). The Father, in a gesture of total self-expression, loves the Son. The Son returns the Father's love fully and completely. The love between Father and Son is the Holy Spirit.

Almost everyone has heard of the famous example of Saint Patrick (385–461 AD), apostle to Ireland. As he evangelized the Irish, Patrick chose the three-leaf clover to symbolize the Trinity. The clover, the plant itself, represents the oneness of God. The three petals illustrate the distinction between the three persons.

Music and Math

For those musically inclined, Saint Ignatius of Loyola's (1491–1556 AD) image may appeal to you. He used the example of three separate musical notes coming together to make one sound, to represent the mystery of the Trinity.

One day Samantha, who happens to be a mathematical whiz, remarked that an equilateral triangle would be a good symbol. "All three sides and angles are equal," she said. "That captures the idea of unity and diversity." This example can be further developed by placing a circle, representing eternity, around the triangle. As if that weren't enough, some even add an "all-seeing" eye inside the triangle.

The class movie buff, Kevin, excitedly cried out, "The *Star Wars* trilogy. Before the last ones were made, *Star Wars*, *The Empire Strikes Back*, and *Return of the Jedi* were all different but had the same story lines."

Whether ancient or new, all these examples give us a small glimpse into the mystery of the Trinity; a mystery that is not be solved, but lived.

JESUS: SYMBOLS FOR ADVENT AND CHRISTMAS

As a child I always dreaded going to church during Advent and Christmas. Wanting to get us more in touch with the season, mom would tell us to go up to the nativity scene and say a few prayers. So each Sunday, slowly and uncomfortably, we went, hoping mom would change her mind. When we reached the nativity, my brothers and I would kneel, say a few quick prayers, and hurry out of church.

The Crèche

Now I know better—not only myself, but the meaning of the nativity scene as well. Though the Feast of the Nativity has long been celebrated by the Church, the nativity scene, or crèche, developed only during the Middle Ages. It was begun by St. Francis of Assisi in the little town of Greccio, Italy, in 1223. This powerful symbol of Jesus' humble birth celebrates the mystery of the incarnation—God taking flesh and living as one with his creation.

In addition to the nativity scene there are other symbols of Jesus associated with Advent and Christmas. They offer an alternative to the seasonal and cultural bombardment of meaningless commercialism. (And we'll look at some of them again in more detail in chapter 6.)

The Advent Wreath

One symbol that we've all come to associate with Advent is the wreath. We find wreaths in our classrooms and homes. Though our attention is often drawn to the evergreen trim and four candles, one for each week of Advent, the most important symbol is the light. During this time of year, the better part of the day is dark. We seem to be surrounded by it. With each passing week of Advent, however, as we get closer to the celebration of Christmas, the ever-increasing light of the Advent wreath reminds and calls us to prepare for Christ, the light of the world.

Two Kinds of Trees

Likewise, at this time of year, trees figure very prominently. One that is often overshadowed by "the great big green one" is the Jesse Tree (Isaiah 11:1). Named after the father of King David and often depicted in stained glass, it portrays the family tree of Jesus. With each successive generation, more branches were added to it—Adam and Eve, Noah, Abraham, Moses, Ruth, Solomon, and so on. Focusing on Jesus' genealogy (Matthew 1:1–17), the symbol testifies both to Jesus as a member of the human family and how long the Jews waited for their much anticipated messiah.

The "other" tree, the Christmas tree, combines a winter solstice celebration of the Germanic peoples with a later medieval morality play. One of the more popular plays revolved around the story of Adam and Eve and the promise of a messiah. A fir tree, adorned with the supposed forbidden apple, served as the Paradise Tree. After their conversion to Christianity, the Germanic peoples took their festival of light and reinterpreted it as representative of the light to come, Jesus the Christ. Bring the two together and over time you have what we know today as the Christmas tree. The challenge is to make the tree more than a mere decoration and to let it speak as the Christian symbol that it is.

Given that Jesus is at the heart of this time of year, it should not be surprising that there are countless symbols expressing both belief in him and beliefs about him.

SACRAMENTS:
LIVING SIGNS OF JESUS' LOVE

Someone once said, "The life of a loving Christian is like a stained glass window. We Christians are called to illustrate the gospel and to let Christ's light and love shine through us." One means for growing in that love is celebrating the sacraments.

Jesus Christ is *the* sacrament of sacraments—the living sign of God's love in our lives. Each of the seven sacraments—through ordinary signs such as washing with water, anointing with oil, eating bread, exchanging vows—is an encounter with the risen Christ, an encounter that enables us to live the gospel more fully and share Christ with those we meet—to be living "stained glass windows."

Ordinary Graces

In our parish church are stained glass windows that depict symbols for each of the sacraments.

BAPTISM Overhead, the first window in our church shows water coming from a shell. This communicates the cleansing power of baptism. This raises the question of where rebirth needs to happen in our own lives and in the lives of those we teach—children and students.

EUCHARIST In the second window, wheat is used to speak of the presence of Christ in the Eucharist. Sometimes grapes are added to represent the body and blood of Christ under both forms. What do we hunger and thirst for? In the area of social justice, how are we feeding others, taking care of their basic needs?

CONFIRMATION The next window has a large white dove, symbolic of the Holy Spirit. Surrounding the dove are seven flames signifying the gifts of the Spirit—wisdom, understanding, counsel, knowledge, piety, fear of the Lord, and fortitude (or courage)— bestowed in their fullness at confirmation. How can we as catechists and teachers (even parents) build up the gifts of our youngsters?

RECONCILIATION When I first saw keys in this window I admit I was stumped until I remembered a passage from Scripture. In Matthew 16:19, after confessing Jesus as messiah, Peter is given the power of the keys, the power to bind and loosen. This authority is exercised when the priest absolves us of our sins. Why is reconciliation difficult, both for us and for those we teach?

MARRIAGE Another window in our church has two interlocking rings (representing union) joined by a cross (speaking to their union in Christ). To what do we need to commit ourselves?

HOLY ORDERS This window combines three symbols: a chalice (representing the priest's power of sacrifice), a stole (speaking of the need for pastoral care), and a book (signifying Jesus' teaching ministry). How do we image Christ through teaching?

ANOINTING OF THE SICK Emphasizing a more positive view of death, the last window has an image of a cloth-draped cross (foreshadowing the end of suffering and of bodily resurrection to come). How have we suffered? Can we help someone right now who is suffering in our midst?

LENT: SYMBOLS OF THE HOLY SPIRIT

How often do we think about the Holy Spirit in connection with Lent? If there is any season that calls for a rediscovery of the Spirit, it is Lent. Unfortunately, with the onslaught of ashes, purple banners, fish fries, and rice bowls, the Spirit's role during Lent is easily forgotten. A sure way to regain it is to focus on the symbols for the Spirit.

Dove: Announcing the Spirit's Presence

Two places where the symbol of the dove figures prominently are in the stories of Noah's Ark and Jesus' baptism. After the great flood, Noah sends out a dove to see if the land is dry or not. Returning with an olive branch, the dove becomes the messenger of good news symbolizing the new creation and peace offered to humanity (Genesis 8:6–12).

When Jesus is baptized in the Jordan, the Spirit descends in the form of a dove and a voice declares Jesus to be God's beloved (Matthew 3:14–17). Righting what Adam had wronged, Jesus likewise becomes the agent of the new creation.

A Season of Re-Creation

Lent, too, is a season of creation and transformation. Catechumens, having taken an extended period of time to explore what it means to be Catholic, ready themselves during the forty days of Lent for initiation into the Church through the sacraments of Baptism, Confirmation, and Eucharist. Through the Spirit these persons will be born anew in Christ. For those already initiated, Lent still offers the opportunity for renewal and recommitment in the

Holy Spirit. When Easter comes we will emerge as a resurrection people.

Wind and Fire: A New Beginning

Even after the resurrection and ascension of Jesus, there was still fear and hesitation among the disciples. That is, until a strong wind filled the room where the apostles were gathered and, in the form of tongues of fire (Acts 2:1–4), the Spirit came upon them. Fear changed to faith. Misery became missionary work as the Spirit enabled them to proclaim Jesus the Christ to all. This new beginning was foreshadowed in the very origins of creation when God's mighty wind (creative Spirit) swept over the waters of chaos bringing forth life (Genesis 1:2). Lent offers this opportunity.

In the midst of our hectic lives, though, the Spirit wanes within us. Schedules become more important than learning, routines more treasured than our relationship with God and others, sports or social obligations more valuable than spiritual growth. Thankfully we can be strengthened and called back by the gifts of the Spirit. Imaged as a seven-branched candlestick holder (also known as a menorah) the gifts of the Spirit include: wisdom, courage, understanding, right judgment, knowledge, reverence, and wonder. These gifts make us more sensitive and able to respond to the action of God in our lives.

Once, while discussing the Spirit in religion class, one of my students said, "I don't know if this sounds right or not, but for me my grandma seems a lot like the Holy Spirit. She's always around even when I don't know it or think about her. When I've had a bad day at school or home, she always has a kind word to cheer me up. Grandma just makes me stronger."

"Kristen," I replied, "you're on the right track."

SYMBOLS OF FAITH:
CONTRADICTORY OR COMPLEMENTARY?

As a symbol of faith, the cross remains the most universal and popular. It is found in our churches. It hangs on our classroom and bedroom walls. We wear it around our necks as jewelry. Perhaps due to its presence just about everywhere, the cross is taken for granted. We forget the starkness and simplicity of its message: Jesus the Christ suffered, died, and rose from the dead.

For Jews and pagans, a savior who was crucified was unthinkable, even laughable (1 Corinthians 1:23). How could victory come from such a defeat? For Christians facing persecution and the very real threat of crucifixion themselves, it was too big a risk to openly display the symbol and take a chance of arrest. It wasn't until around the fifth century that the cross began to emerge as a public expression of faith linking Good Friday and Easter Sunday.

For the Marathon of Faith

Though it may be hard to consider during certain times of the year, there is a symbol from spring that can help us realize what faith is all about—the butterfly. As it slowly crawls from place to place, the caterpillar goes unrecognized and unappreciated for the creature it is to become. It will then go inside a shell and hide from the world. Over time, though, an amazing transformation takes place. What was once an ugly "worm" becomes a beautiful butterfly. So, too, it is with persons of faith. Still just learning how to walk on the spiritual path, we're uncertain where we're going and may shut ourselves off from others for fear of embarrassment and failure. Yet, at some point, we leave the shadow of the tomb and enter into the light of the resurrection.

Another ancient symbol of faith for Christians and the Church is the ark (or ship). From the earliest years right up to this day, the followers of Jesus have had to sail troubled waters. Whether it's persecution by others, internal disagreements, or comfortable complacency, smooth seas quickly turn to windy storms where it's hard to stay afloat. The apostles experienced this when they were in a boat during a storm on the Sea of Galilee, and Jesus calmed the storm.

However long we've been on the road, the faith journey is still very tiring. As soon as we catch our breath, a new challenge comes along. The road of faith may seem long, but the direction becomes clear with these symbols of faith.

FROM EAGLE TO OX: THE GOSPEL SYMBOLS

One Saturday night as my wife, my daughter, and I entered the church in my wife's hometown, our daughter's attention was drawn up to the ceiling.

There, in each corner, was a symbol of one of the four evangelists—a human, lion, ox, and eagle. I could only smile when she looked at me excitedly and said, "Daddy, look. It's a lion. Rrroar!" For her it appeared to be a "theological zoo," while in truth each symbol served as a summary of one of the gospels.

The symbols are drawn from the Book of Ezekiel. There, in the opening chapter, the prophet describes a vision of four living creatures. Human in form, each one has four faces and four wings. A similar vision takes place in the Book of Revelation (4:7).

The Good News in Brief

As educators, we're always on the lookout for things that can take something complex and complicated and make it understandable. The symbols of the gospels serve just that purpose. For if you know what the symbol means, you've gone a long way in realizing the central message of that specific gospel. The challenge then becomes one of helping children go beyond the symbol, that *Cliff Note* of information, to read and experience the gospel.

Matthew: The Human Figure

At first glance Matthew's genealogy of Jesus doesn't seem to be that important. It's just a list of names, a long list of names: Abraham, Isaac, Jacob, Judah…. Matthew's genealogy is there for a reason, however. It roots Jesus within human history and speaks to his Jewish ancestry. It is for this reason that Matthew's symbol is a man (often pictured winged).

Mark: The Lion

The gospel opens with John the Baptist's lionesque "roar." His voice is "of one crying out in the desert: 'Prepare the way of the Lord, make straight his paths.'" John even looked the part with his tangled mane of hair and camel's hair clothes. Interestingly, long ago people used to believe that lions were born dead. It was thought that the voice of the lion raised the cubs to life on the third day. Such was the goal of John, accomplished through Jesus, to bring life to Israel. Tradition also accords St. Mark the symbol of the lion in that the gospel speaks of Jesus' royal dignity.

Luke: The Ox

Here the story of Jesus begins not in the little town of Bethlehem or the barren desert, but in the busy and bustling Temple in Jerusalem. There Zechariah, husband of Elizabeth and soon-to-be father of John the Baptist, is fulfilling his priestly duties by ritually sacrificing animals. One such animal was the ox. This foreshadows the atoning and sacrificial nature of Jesus' life, death, and resurrection.

John: The Eagle

When speaking of Jesus, John's gospel uses exalted language: "In the beginning was the Word, and the Word was with God, and the Word was God" (1:1). Unlike the other three, or synoptic, gospels, which focus more on Jesus' humanity, John gives us insight into Jesus' divinity. For this reason, the symbol of the eagle has come to be associated with this gospel. The eagle, like John the Evangelist, flies to the heights and gazes piercingly into the mystery that is Christ's divinity.

Over the years, these symbols have found expression in paintings, been carved into pulpits, and have adorned objects of worship. Taken as a whole the images are representative of Christ's life and point to his incarnation, sacrificial death, triumphant resurrection, and ascension into heaven.

QUESTIONS FOR
REVIEW AND REFLECTION

- Your meeting space can help youngsters develop imagination and symbolic thinking. Which objects in it are open to many different interpretations? Which objects are limited in meaning?

- Reflect on what gifts of the Spirit you're using now. Which ones do you still need to "unwrap"?

- What does the cross symbolize for you? Where are there crosses in your life?

ACTIVITIES

- In a way we are living symbols. As a means of sharing who we are with one another, ask each student to bring in an object that reveals a dimension of their personality not readily perceived.

- Using family pictures, magazines, and newspapers, make a collage showing the Spirit at work in our lives. In the center put images of the three primary symbols—dove, wind, fire—surrounding them with images of the gifts of the Spirit in action.

- Make a cover for your classroom or family bible, or your religion book, using one or all of the symbols of the four evangelists.

PRAYER STARTER

Read Genesis 18 (the story of Abraham's visitors) with your class. If you have a copy of it, show them Andrei Rublev's icon of the scene. Take some time now to consider what this passage and image say about the ultimate mystery and symbol of our faith—the Trinity.

CHAPTER 2

Symbols of a Church, Our Home of Faith

THE CHURCH: GOD'S HOME, OUR HOME

Maria sat quietly at her desk waiting for the bell to ring. She'd just moved from Texas. Not knowing anyone, she felt a little nervous, even scared. When she heard the bell, Maria remembered the words her mom said, "Don't worry dear. You'll make friends soon. Hang in there."

"Good morning class. Before we get started," Mrs. Burns announced, "I'd like to introduce our new student, Maria Cruz. Would anyone like to show her around school at lunch today?" Leslie and Kyle raised their hands.

At lunch, Leslie and Kyle took Maria to all the usual places. Along the way, Maria and Leslie discovered they both shared an interest in gymnastics. Kyle even played the piano like Maria did. At the end of the tour they stopped at the parish church next door.

For a moment Maria felt like she was back home. The baptismal font was in the same location as the one in her old parish. Straight ahead was the altar and close by was the lectern. Light shone through the stained glass windows.

Maria told her new friends, "Saint Patrick's is a lot bigger than my old church." They laughed and said, "Come on, we'd better hurry before lunch recess is over." Maria was beginning to feel like she belonged.

Community and Participation

Church is home—both God's and ours. This chapter will focus on the symbols of the church—the stained glass windows and statues, the ambo (lectern), the altar, the Stations of the Cross, the baptismal font, and the assembly. Two themes will guide us.

The first is that whenever we talk about "the church" we're referring just as much, if not more so, to the people who gather there as to the building itself. It must not be forgotten, though, that the building is a powerful symbol and testament to the faith of the community. In the history of the Church these buildings have ranged from private homes to basilicas (based on the public meeting halls of the Romans) and grand Gothic cathedrals. In their own way, through the worship and praise of countless persons and generations, all have become sacred places.

The second is that knowledge of symbols increases the likelihood of participation in the Church's life and liturgy. Most people will agree that the wider culture does little to reinforce the Catholic identity of our children. Some would say, what with music, television, and computers, secular culture has an unfair advantage. It's all the more important then that we make use of the liturgy and its storehouse of faith symbols.

If our children know the good word that comes from the lectionary proclaimed from the ambo, they will be able to resist "other" words. If they see the light shining through the saints in the stained glass windows, they will be more likely to choose them as their heroes instead of our culture's "person of the week." If they know the banquet that is offered to them on the altar, they will think again—the next time they dine at some fast-food place—about what really nourishes.

The church and its symbols, when communicated effectively, really do shape our faith. Even more so, they shape our lives.

STAINED GLASS AND STATUES: LETTING THE LIGHT IN

One day a mother was spending a few minutes of reflection and prayer in a church with her young son, Brendan. Never having been inside this church before, Brendan's eyes were immediately drawn to the church's large stained glass windows. Overcome with excitement, he tugged at his mother's jacket wanting to know more about them.

Instinctively, she responded, "They're saints." Soon Brendan was at his mother again. "Mommy, Mommy!" Irritated by this distraction, she quickly asked, "What?" To which he responded, "I know what saints do, Mommy. They let the light in."

The role of saints was communicated to the young boy through the symbol of stained glass. Without even realizing it, he got right to the heart of a key Catholic characteristic—sacramentality. Though quite a long word, it simply means that the supposedly distant and remote God is made personal and concrete through ordinary actions and words (and people—the saints).

Stained Glass Windows

Stained glass is one such ordinary thing. It emerged with the great Gothic cathedrals of the Middle Ages. During a time when few people could read or write, these churches took on the role of "bibles in stone." When people came to these churches, as we still do to ours today, they saw characters from the Hebrew Scriptures, scenes from the life of Jesus, and images of the saints and Mary. The Christian journey that they struggled to live daily was being paralleled in the pictures above them.

The Meaning of Statues

Statues are another way we can connect to the journey of faith. They all remind us of the larger faith story that we are a part of. Like our familiar family photographs and albums, they tell us where we've come from and where we might be headed. This helps us realize who we are.

As important and beautiful as stained glass and statues are, they are not ends, or idols, unto themselves. They exist to bring us into deeper relationship with God through Jesus the Christ.

Taken together, stained-glass windows and statues speak to the very Catholic belief in the communion of saints. It attests to the union that exists between the living and the dead, in a relationship that transcends time and space. Praying to and asking the saints to intercede on our behalf is very much a part of Catholic devotional life.

THE WORD OF GOD:
THE AMBO AND THE LECTIONARY

"All right, Cara, it's time for bed."

"But Daddy," she replies, "we need to read a story first."

Oops! How could I forget story time? With that our ritual begins. She picks one or two of her favorite books. Then she climbs up and joins me at the foot of the bed. It's our special place. With the pillows perfectly positioned,

Cara and I read our books together. Their words and stories touch our lives and bring us closer together. I wouldn't miss it for the world.

The Ambo

The church too has a special reading place. It goes by several different names—ambo, lectern, pulpit. (Though at one time there were distinctions between the terms, for the most part they are used interchangeably today.) Here the word of God is proclaimed through Scripture, sung through psalms, and explained through homilies. The words spoken from the ambo are not ancient words with no bearing on the present. Through them God's very self is revealed. God is communicating with us now, revealing God's self anew. Indicating its importance, the first part of Mass is called the Liturgy of the Word.

For this reason, though at first it may sound strange to "Catholic ears," the ambo must be reverenced and respected just as the altar is. This should be reflected in its architecture as well. In this way, the close relationship between the altar and ambo will be realized and lived. As the faithful have long known, the "table of the word" leads to the "table of the Eucharist." Fed by the word of God proclaimed from the ambo, we are better prepared to receive Christ's body.

The Word as "Advent"

Similarly, Advent is a time of preparation. During this season we're called to become more aware of the comings of Jesus the Christ, the "word made flesh." As John's Gospel reads: "In the beginning was the Word, and the Word was with God, and the Word was God" (1:1). Jesus came not only 2,000 years ago; he also comes to us daily, and will come again in the future.

What's that Book?

I remember one time, early in the year right after our first all-school liturgy, one non-Catholic youngster asked, "What's that book you bring into Mass and place on the lectern? Is it the bible?" "You're close," I said. "Actually, it's called the lectionary. A lot of people confuse it with the bible, though." The lectionary is the book that contains the three-year cycle of readings proclaimed at Mass. The purpose of it is to give us greater exposure to the word of God. Generally speaking, the first reading comes from the Hebrew Scriptures. This is followed by a responsorial psalm. The second reading usually comes from one of the New Testament letters, or the Acts of the Apostles. The final reading comes from one of the Gospels.

Shortly after that first youngster's question, another one asked, "Why do Catholics rub their faces before they read the Gospel?" A smile came to my face. How confusing some symbols must be to those who don't understand them (this includes some Catholics!). Connected with both the ambo and the lectionary is the symbolic gesture of signing one's forehead, lips, and chest before the Gospel is read. The words, I told him, are: "May the Lord be in my mind, on my lips, and in my heart." In making this prayer we are opening our whole being, not just a part of it, to the word of God. Sure beats making smudge marks!

Such is the potential and power of the word of God!

THE ALTAR: THE CHURCH'S DINNER TABLE

Looking back, I don't remember how this particular group of youngsters got on the subject. I just happened to be passing by their desks and overheard them talking about what room in their houses they liked the most. The answers varied. One boy said his bedroom was his favorite room. Another, the basement. Then, accompanied by a chorus of laughter and "Me too's," someone else replied, "The bathroom."

At this point, I thought it was a good idea to enter the conversation. Rather than tell them to get busy on something constructive, though, I thought I'd challenge them a bit. "Since we know what the favorite place in your home is, how about telling me what's the most important?" It appeared I'd stumped them. After a few moments however, Kevin, the quieter of the three, said, "I know. The kitchen. That's where my family all comes together to the table to eat and share our day with one another." I was impressed.

The Center of a Meal

In a real way, the altar is the Church's dinner table. I'm sure you've either said or heard the saying, "You can learn a lot about someone by looking at their furnishings." Most Catholic churches, given the placement and size of their altars, communicate that the altar is the most important piece of furniture. For it is there that we gather as one family in faith to tell the story of Jesus' life, death, and resurrection.

From the Last Supper to this upcoming Sunday, Jesus continues to invite us to break bread and share drink with him. In doing so, we're not only nourished physically and spiritually, but the story of Jesus is told anew. In this light, the table of the Lord stands as a reminder and challenges us to model the fellowship of Jesus to others. Whether it's in our family, school, or neighborhood, there are surely people out there in need of a seat at the banquet table.

It's Not About Us

One thing we have to do when we're at table with others is to share or to sacrifice. The phrases vary. "Scoot over." "Pass the vegetables, please." "Help your sister." "Cut me a piece of pie." And the dreaded, "Clean up." All indicate that we're a part of a community.

The same is true when we approach the altar of the Lord. In response to the one who sacrificed his very life for love of neighbor, we're called to give rather than get. Yet, our culture's rugged individualism fights against this realization. The altar serves as an antidote to this mentality.

Not unlike the Jews who presented their prized animals as offerings to the Lord, we approach the altar mindful of how blessed we are. It's only natural, then, to ask ourselves what we can give back to Jesus who has given so much to us.

Just as the priest will kiss or bow before the altar, so too can our children bow or genuflect in front of it as a symbol of Christ's presence in our midst.

The paten and chalice are often associated with the altar. The paten, or bread plate, holds the eucharistic bread that will become our Lord's body. The chalice, or cup, holds the wine that will become our Lord's blood.

As he has done from the beginning, Jesus calls us to his table to share in the feast.

STATIONS OF THE CROSS: WALKING IN THE LORD'S FOOTSTEPS

"Any intentions?" I asked as we began prayer. Sarah raised her hand. "I'd like to pray for my grandparents," she said. "They're going on a pilgrimage to the Holy Land soon. I hope they have a safe trip." Events in that part of the world suggested cause for her concern.

A couple of weeks later, as she left class, I asked her how her grandparents' trip was. With a look of disappointment on her face, she told me that they had not been able to go. "It was cancelled because of all the violence over there. They're going to reschedule it when things calm down. Their group is going to do the Stations of the Cross at their parish instead."

Unable to go to the Holy Land in person, Sarah's grandparents were able to make a spiritual pilgrimage in the footsteps of the Lord by means of the Stations of the Cross (also known as the "Way of the Cross" and *Via Dolorosa*, "the Sorrowful Way").

A Popular Pilgrimage

Almost from the very beginning of Christianity, pilgrims went to the Holy Land to visit the places made holy during Jesus' final days. They sought to walk in his footsteps, beginning with Jesus' condemnation by Pilate and ending with his entombment. The popularity of the pilgrimage as a devotion grew greatly during the Crusades (11th–13th centuries). It was especially promoted by the Franciscans after they gained custody of the Holy Land in the 14th century. The Christians who went there, whether as soldiers or pilgrims, brought this practice back home with them.

Eventually, the Holy Land was taken over by Muslims, which made it difficult for pilgrims to go there in person. Thus, as a kind of substitute for those who could not afford the financial expense or undergo the physical challenges and other risks of an actual pilgrimage, the Stations of the Cross came into being. Over time private outdoor shrines, then indoor shrines that depicted the stations found their way into parish churches.

Part of the devotion's success is due to its flexibility. It can be celebrated either individually or communally (preferably it is celebrated by the community). It also exercises the imagination as each participant is asked to meditate upon the various stations. These meditations remind us of Jesus' suffering in his Passion, but also asks us to consider how Jesus may be suffering in his people today.

Changes in Form and Celebration

Over time the form of the stations has varied. They have been depicted with simple crosses, elaborate carved stone or wood, modern abstract art, beautiful mosaics, dramatic paintings, and pressed metals. Whatever the style, all invite us to journey with Jesus during his last days and final hours. It makes sense then that the Stations of the Cross would eventually become synonymous with Lent. It is during this season that we are encouraged to turn away from sin and walk with Jesus.

As with their form, so too their number has changed over time. Today the number of stations stands at fourteen. Many refer to Scripture passages, while some, like the story of Veronica wiping the face of Jesus, depend more on tradition. Recognizing the fullness of the paschal mystery, some celebrations have added a fifteenth station—the Resurrection. This reminds us that life, not death, is the final answer.

BAPTISMAL FONT AND PASCHAL CANDLE: THROUGH DEATH TO NEW LIFE

Several months ago our son was baptized. Gathered together with family and friends, Brendan was welcomed into the community of faith. Thinking ahead as to how my wife and I, along with Brendan's godparents, can help our son on his journey of faith, two symbols stand out from that day: the baptismal font and the paschal candle.

From Tomb to Womb

There to the side of the altar was the baptismal font. It is at one and the same time the tomb and womb of the Church. Water can be destructive and deadly, yet also life-giving. In baptism, we die to a life of sin. Washed with these same waters, though, we rise to new life.

In fact, the word baptism comes from the Greek *baptizein*, which means to "immerse" or to "plunge." Transformation, resurrection, Easter indeed! The words said at the blessing of the water capture this process well: "May all who are buried with Christ in the death of baptism rise also with him to newness of life."

Another symbol reminding us of our baptism—blessing ourselves with holy water from side-door fonts—can become routine and mechanical. We need to remind ourselves and our young people that through this gesture we further enter into the life, death, and resurrection of Jesus—a simple act, profoundly meaningful. This serves to remind us that Easter is always nearby, if only we'd recognize it.

From Darkness to Light

Right next to the baptismal font was the paschal, or Easter, candle. Its size dwarfed all the other candles in the church. It symbolizes that in the midst of darkness and sin Christ is the light of the world (John 8:12). From the paschal candle, another candle was lighted by Brendan's godparents to show that it is their responsibility to help guide and light Brendan's path. It also shows that the child himself becomes a "child of light."

During the fifty days of the Easter season, the candle remains in the church sanctuary. After the season is over, it is placed by the baptismal font and lighted again for celebrations of the sacrament. It is also placed beside coffins at funerals. This foreshadows Christ's continued presence and victory over death.

THE ASSEMBLY:
THE PRESENCE OF GOD IN OUR MIDST

Sunday after Sunday we go. Upon entering church our eyes are drawn to the symbols of the altar and the ambo, the stained glass windows and the statues, and the baptismal font and the tabernacle. That's all there is, right? We've been there so often we usually miss what is considered by many to be the most important symbol of God's presence—the assembly.

"But all we do is just sit, stand, and kneel," my youngsters will say. The role they experience when participating in liturgy is far too often one that seems insignificant and irrelevant. This echoes the experience of many older Catholics who saw their role as one of "pray, pay, and obey."

Yet the assembly, gathered as one body, joined in prayer, song, and worship, powerfully communicates the presence of God in our midst. This was one of the more important teachings of the Second Vatican Council. Its *Constitution on the Sacred Liturgy* recalls the multiple presences of Christ in the liturgy: the sacrifice of the Mass, the person of the priest, the eucharistic species of bread and wine, the other sacraments, and the proclaimed word (#7). The document ends by stating: "He is present...when the Church prays and sings, for he promised: 'Where two or three are gathered for my sake, there I am in the midst of them' (Matthew 18:20)."

For a community long focused on the Eucharist as the presence of Christ, this invitation has slowly begun to take root. Our celebration of the body and blood of Christ should bring with it the recognition that we too are the body of Christ, the people of God. As Saint Paul reminds us, we, and not just the buildings, are also temples of the Holy Spirit (see 1 Corinthians 3:16–17; 6:19). God dwells within us as persons and community!

Sharing the Eucharist with the World

As important as the Eucharist is, even more so is the realization that the Eucharist must live in us as the people of God so that we may share it with the world. In that way we too will become the living sacrifice, the living word, and the living food of the Mass for others.

It only makes sense, then, that we respond with "full, conscious, and active participation." "Such participation by the Christian people," the *Constitution on the Sacred Liturgy* says, "is their right and duty by reason of their baptism." Even when the assembly area, or nave, is empty, it communicates that the people of God are now out in the world making it holy.

The assembly concretely shows that we are a Pentecost people. Having ascended to heaven, Jesus the Christ has charged all baptized believers, empowered by the Holy Spirit, to share his good news with the world. No longer do we look outside ourselves for Christ's presence, but rejoice that Christ is within us (see Acts 2:1–4).

QUESTIONS FOR
REVIEW AND REFLECTION

- Like stained glass windows, how do we let the light of Jesus shine through us?

- Which part of the Liturgy of the Word speaks to you the most: Scripture readings, psalms, or homily? Why?

- Both the baptismal font and paschal candle recall sig-

nificant stories of faith. Talk about the stories in your
life and the lives of your young people that speak to the
themes of death to life and darkness to light.

- If we are the body of Christ and the Eucharist lives in us,
what difference should this make in our lives? How can
we concretely share the Eucharist with the world?

ACTIVITIES

- Are your youngsters familiar with the stained glass windows and statues in your parish church? Take them for a
tour, talk about the meaning of the windows and statues.

- Design a Stations of the Cross for your classroom.
Materials needed: colored paper, magazines, crayons,
colored pencils, scissors, glue, etc. Divide your class into
groups of two or three. Depending on the size of the
class, groups may have more than one station assigned
to them. Have each group visually/artistically present
their station(s). With each station have the group provide both a reflection/prayer that brings together the
station in its historical setting and its application today.
When each group is finished, hang up the stations in
your room or a more suitable place and enact the stations with your class.

PRAYER STARTER

At home or school, in the kitchen or dining room, tables
serve as a potential symbol of community. It's good to consider who sits at the table with us and drinks from the cup.
Who is missing? What resolution do we need to make to
become more inclusive persons and communities?

CHAPTER 3

Symbolic Persons from Scripture

THE FOUNDATIONAL SYMBOL: ADAM AND EVE

"But what about the dinosaurs?" I asked my mom. "Where were they at the time of Adam and Eve?" As a young child that was one of my big theological questions. I was stumped. And as any good, unknowing parent usually does, my mom tried to change the subject as quickly as possible.

I didn't know it at the time, but I had literalized the story. I had taken what was meant to be symbolic and figurative and made it historical and scientific. (As we discuss the symbols of the Hebrew Scriptures, I am aware that most adolescents are at a very concrete, literal stage in their life.) In the process, I missed out on the real meaning of the story.

I have since learned that the Hebrew Scriptures are full of symbols. Their stories and characters can even be looked at as prefiguring the coming of Jesus the Christ. One story that surely illustrates this is the creation story (Genesis 1:1—2:4a and 2:4b—3:24) and the characters of Adam and Eve.

Who Are They?

In these two people we discover something about our very selves—that we are made in the image and likeness of God (Genesis 1:27). Adam (Hebrew for "man" or "human") is not meant to be taken for a specific name, but rather refers to humanity collectively. Likewise, Eve (Hebrew for "the mother of all the living") speaks to our common union as human beings. Despite strong evidence to the contrary, we are all one family.

How quickly things unravel.

Called to be living images of God, Adam and Eve (you and I) soon desire to be gods themselves. The serpent (now a classic symbol of evil and temptation) didn't need to wait long for takers on his fruit snack (Genesis 3). The fall comes quickly. Soon, the game of "he said, she said" is played out. Where once they enjoyed Eden, "garden of delight" (it's not a place you'll find on the map), now their time is spent on the outside looking in.

We know all too well what often happens to the best-laid plans. Family, job, friendships are no different. We intend to establish good relationships and communication, but they often seem to break down before they begin.

O Happy Fault!

It may be helpful at this point to repeat something we say during the Easter Vigil: "O happy fault, O necessary sin of Adam, which gained for us so great a redeemer." God does not let the example of Adam and Eve stand.

God knew there had to be another way to repair the broken relationship that resulted from the sin of Adam. The Incarnation—God made flesh in Jesus of Nazareth—was the answer. As Saint Paul says: "For if by that one person's transgression the many died, how much more did the grace of God and the most gracious gift of the one person Jesus Christ overflow for the many" (Romans 5:15).

Adam and Eve function, then, as foundational symbols. They tell us who we are called to be (images of God) and yet who we are (fallen images in need of redemption). Experiencing our likeness to Adam and Eve, we are called to become more like the new Adam, Jesus Christ.

NOAH AND THE ARK: SYMBOL OF UNCONDITIONAL LOVE

Have you ever had that one particular, challenging child? You can't do anything right. The session is either too boring or too long. The assignments you give are either too easy or too hard. Finally, at the same time, the room itself is too cold and too hot. You just can't catch a break! But by now you're in no mood to give one in return. An icy stalemate has been reached.

Now picture God. With the best of intentions God brought forth the wondrous act of creation. The crowning achievement, or so God thought, was humanity. Problem, though: Adam and Eve didn't listen. Cain and Abel didn't get along. Then—and this shouldn't surprise us—the whole lot of humanity took a turn for the worse. What to do?

The Flood

In a moment of frustration and exasperation God decides to destroy all of creation with a flood (Genesis 6:11–13). The thinking seemed to be, "Let's just start all over. Besides I couldn't do any worse and they deserve it!" Likewise, on our own days when nothing seems to work, we too may feel like starting all over again. Thankfully, wiser heads prevail. In the end the story of Noah and the Ark is not about the flood (the exacting of punishment) but the rainbow (the promise of renewal).

Though you'll never find the conversation in your bible, I often picture God apologizing to Noah after the flood. "It didn't work," God says. "What?" asks Noah. "The flood—punishment," replies God. "From now on, to remind myself that punishment is not the answer, after each rainstorm a bow will appear in the sky. It will be there as a reminder that the only way is love" (Genesis 8:20–22).

The Covenant

A covenant—not a legal agreement but a relationship—is established. It doesn't get God and humanity out of a jam so much as it charts a new vision for creation. Recognizing the sinful condition of human beings, God decides that if it comes down to choosing punishment or compassion, compassion will win hands down. Through it all God demonstrates the principle that punishment or fear may stop a child's or class' behavior for a while, but if you want lasting change, love is the only answer.

For me the story of Noah symbolizes God's unconditional love of humanity. Whether one is green, a first-year catechist, or a seasoned veteran, this is not always easy to put into practice. You may even be able to put forth numerous exceptions to the rule. However, God's love is the model and challenge we have before us. In a world and culture that demands punishment, how can we display a love that is both accountable and merciful? The answer: the story of Noah leads us to the person of Jesus and the example of those who followed in his footsteps—among whom the first is his mother, Mary, as the following quote from Saint Francis de Sales illustrates. "If the early Christians were described as having one heart and soul, on account of their perfect mutual love; if Saint Paul was alive to self no longer, but Christ lived in him by reason of the close union of heart between him and his Master... how much truer it is to say that the Blessed Virgin and her Son had only one heart, one soul, one life; that his holy Mother was living, though not with her own life...Christ was alive in her!"

ABRAHAM: SYMBOL OF THE JOURNEY

I'd already been in the fourth grade for a couple of weeks when I heard the news. My dad had been offered a new job. It sounded like we would be moving soon, not just to a new house but to a new state. Everything that I'd known and felt comfortable with would soon be gone. Little did I know at the time that this situation had been shared by one of the great persons of faith—Abraham.

When we first encounter Abraham in Scripture, he, too, is moving (by invitation of God): "Go forth from the land of your kinfolk and from your father's house to a land that I will show you" (Genesis 12:1). When he should have been enjoying the fruits of his retirement, Abraham and his wife Sarah left the security of their country, home, and inheritance. They set out for the unknown.

What sustained them was the promise of a son and that Abraham would be the father of many nations. In fact, God proclaimed: "I will make of you a great nation, and I will bless you; I will make your name great, so that you will be a blessing" (Genesis 12:2).

After a while, though, Abraham felt as if he were getting the short end of the stick: "O Lord God, what good will your gifts be, if I keep being childless...?" (Genesis 15:2). Desiring an heir, Sarah allowed Abraham to have intercourse with her maid-servant, Hagar. This resulted in the birth of a son, Ishmael. Rather than bringing relief, however, Ishmael's birth brought tension. Eventually, the couple's hopes were fulfilled as Sarah and Abraham were told that they would have a son. At this news, given all that they had gone through, Sarah laughed—hence the name "Isaac," which means, "he laughs."

Holy Days of the Journey

The season of Advent reminds us of the "leaps of faith" we need to take in our own lives. Sometimes in the midst of all the "business" of the season we lose sight of the presence of God. During these times we may become selfish and inconsiderate, thinking only of ourselves.

Here the example of Mary, the mother of Jesus, has much to teach us. Her acceptance of the angel Gabriel's invitation to be the mother of the Messiah required a leap of faith, a profound change. Little did she know what she was getting herself into when she replied: "Behold, I am the handmaid of the Lord. May it be done to me according to your word" (Luke 1:38). Her life was intimately connected with the spiritual journey of her son, Jesus, from the stable in Bethlehem to the foot of the cross outside Jerusalem.

The lives of Abraham, Mary—and our own lives—are all marked by the journey.

JACOB: SYMBOL OF THE UNEXPECTED GOD

Picture this: two brothers at odds since birth. One was robbed of his inheritance. The mother was willingly involved and encouraged the deception. Sibling death-threats followed. Fearing for his life, the favored son was exiled to foreign lands. Finally, in the end, there was a touching reconciliation.

What is this? Daytime television at its finest? A new prime-time show? No. It's the story of Jacob, son of Isaac, and one of our faith's great patriarchs.

Trouble from the Beginning

While pregnant with Jacob and Esau, Rebekah was told by the Lord that "the older shall serve the younger" (Genesis 25:23). In a society that privileged the eldest brother this was troubling, to say the least. According to plan though, Jacob was born gripping the heel of his brother Esau.

With the competition heating up, Jacob looked for any chance he could get. One time, after being out in the wilderness, Esau returned home starving. He called out to his brother for some food to quench his appetite. Jacob seized the opportunity: no birthright, no food. Esau replied, "I'm on the point of dying. What good will any birthright do me?" With that Jacob obtained Esau's birthright for a little bread and lentil soup (Genesis 25:29–34).

The ultimate deception, though, came at the deathbed of his now near-blind father, Isaac. Isaac, fearing the end of his life was near, sent Esau out to get food for the meal at which he would bestow his special blessing, the birthright, on his first-born son, Esau. Overhearing this, Rebekah called for her favorite, Jacob. She gave him Esau's clothes, the hair of animals to cover his body (because Esau was a hairy man), and an appetizing dish.

With all of his bases covered, Jacob approached his father. Surprised at his quick return and sudden change in voice, Isaac tested him to make sure it was Esau. He felt the hairy hands and smelt the fragrance of his clothes. It had to be Esau. With that Isaac imparted his blessing on Jacob (Genesis 27).

Contending with the Divine

Fearing that his brother would kill him, Jacob went into exile in the land of his uncle Laban. There some say he got his just deserts. In love with Laban's younger daughter Rachel, Jacob was tricked into marrying his eldest daughter, Leah. After some twenty years of toil, Jacob is told by the Lord to return home.

The evening before he meets his brother, Esau, Jacob is full of mixed emotions. Deciding whether to return to his home or not, he spends some time alone. It is here that he meets a man with whom he wrestles until the break of dawn. Besting the man, Jacob would not let go until he bestowed a blessing. The man, later identified as an angel, does so by giving Jacob a new name, *Israel*, which means "one who has contended with divine beings" (Genesis 32:23–32). The following day, despite his fears, Jacob's meeting with Esau brings reconciliation and a new beginning.

Looking at this story in light of the mystery of the Incarnation brings an added dimension to it. We also encounter God in unexpected ways and places. God doesn't favor the "winners" but rather challenges our expectations. The lowly find blessings while those in high places are humbled. In the Incarnation, too, we find our struggle with the divine beings. It just doesn't make sense (in human terms) that God has thought so highly of us as to become one with us. Yet, this is the reality we celebrate as Christians.

MOSES: SYMBOL OF LIBERATION

In my hometown of Cincinnati, the National Underground Railroad and Freedom Center stands on the banks of the Ohio River separating the North and the South. It commemorates a chapter in our nation's history that we would rather forget—slavery. This land of the free and home of the brave was once a place of bondage and oppression. One name that many associate with the Underground Railroad, the network of houses and people that helped slaves move without detection from the South to the North, is Harriet Tubman. For her vital role in freeing escaped slaves she was given the name "Moses." How well these people knew the person of Moses and the story of Exodus. How much they needed it. For us today, it is no different.

Just when it seems to the Hebrew people that all is lost and that evil is going to win the day, God sends a liberator, Moses, to free them from their captivity in Egypt. Though we may remember more vividly the ten plagues, the parting of the sea, and the giving of the Ten Commandments, perhaps the pivotal story in the Book of Exodus is the burning bush.

The Burning Bush

It's a question that we may not want to ask, but can't avoid: "Who am I?" Moses faces this question. Raised in the court of Pharaoh, a "prince of Egypt," Moses still feels uncomfortable. While visiting the forced labor camps of the Hebrews, he witnesses an Egyptian slave driver strike and whip a Hebrew slave. Moses is so outraged by this act of inhumanity that he kills the Egyptian. Realizing what he has done, having affirmed the dignity and value of a Hebrew, a slave, Moses flees to the desert. Even there, though, he cannot escape the question: "Who am I?"

One day while tending sheep, he sees the unbelievable, a bush engulfed with flames but not consumed. There, on Mount Sinai, Moses has his conversion experience, a "burning bush" experience if you will. No longer is Moses able to evade the question of his own identity. God reveals God's very self to him: "I am who am" (Exodus 3:14). From that experience, Moses affirms his Hebrew heritage and casts aside his cultural Egyptian upbringing. The long march to freedom begins.

An interesting and important twist to this history is the role of women in it. Without them the Exodus would never have happened. If the midwives had obeyed the command of Pharaoh to kill all newborn male Hebrews, there would have been no Exodus. If Moses' mother had not hidden her son and later sent him down the Nile, no Exodus. If Pharaoh's daughter had let the papyrus basket float by, no Exodus. Finally, if Moses' sister, Miriam, hadn't emerged from the reeds and offered to find someone to nurse the infant Moses, no Exodus. But there was an Exodus, chiefly due to the role of women.

Invitation to Freedom

Though we're not enslaved in chains and forced to make bricks without straw, slavery still exists today in one form or another. We're all in need of a Moses to free us from our Pharaohs. Best symbolized during the season of Lent, the journey to Easter, to resurrection, to conversion awaits and with it the familiar echoes of "pray, fast, give alms."

As a Jew, Jesus had the person of Moses and the story of the Exodus constantly on his mind and lips. Prior to his crucifixion and death, he even celebrated a Passover meal with his disciples. He then invited his disciples to experience the saving presence of God in their lives, calling them out of the slavery of sin and into the freedom of God's friendship.

Easily summarized and spoken, yet difficult to realize at any time of the liturgical year: Be free!

DAVID: SYMBOL OF CONTRADICTION

I don't know about you, but I like rooting for the underdog. Maybe that's why every time the baseball playoffs come around, I cheer for the Chicago Cubs.

When we first encounter David in Scripture, if anything he is an underdog. Due to Saul's disobedience, the prophet Samuel travels to Bethlehem in search of a new king (1 Samuel 16). There he meets Jesse and his sons. Going against custom, Samuel secretly anoints David, the youngest son, as king. This supposed lowly and simple shepherd would become a giant known as "a man after God's own heart" (1 Samuel 13:14).

A Changing Relationship

Soon David finds himself in the camp of Saul. At various times, he soothes the king's depression by playing the harp. The action that brings him to everyone's attention, though, is his fight with Goliath (1 Samuel 17). Goliath cuts an intimidating figure. Armed only with five smooth stones, David meets Goliath in battle. When they encounter one another, David takes a stone from his bag and slings it at the Philistine. Goliath is hit squarely on the forehead and falls dead. David and the Israelites are victorious. The underdog has won!

Unfortunately, this does not bring King Saul and David closer together but drives them further apart. Later David returns from a successful campaign against the Philistines. Hearing his people sing, "Saul has killed his thousands, and David his ten thousands," Saul grows jealous and seeks to take care of this "enemy of the state." Saul continually seeks David's life until Saul's own death during a battle with the Philistine army (1 Samuel 30).

David Becomes King

After Saul's death David becomes king of Israel. He brings the Ark of the Covenant into Jerusalem. Rather than have David build a temple to house the Ark, God tells David that he will build him an everlasting kingdom, a royal dynasty (2 Samuel 7). Like many a leader, however, David gets caught up with his successes—personal, military, political, and religious—and forgets the role God has played in his life.

It all comes to a head in his affair with Bathsheba (2 Samuel 11). Not only does he have an affair with her, but when he finds out that she is pregnant, David arranges the death of her husband, Uriah. Before David gets off scot free, however, the prophet Nathan tells him a parable. In it a rich man steals and kills a poor man's lamb. David is incensed at the action of the rich man and says he should be killed. At which point Nathan says: "You are the man!" (2 Samuel 12).

Forced to realize his sins, David repents. It is not without cost, however, as tragedy and division will confront his family.

"Turn Away from Sin"

It is good to know and remind ourselves that God works with us despite our failings, weaknesses, and sins. Resurrection, rebirth, and transformation await us all. We are all called forth from the tomb of sin to the womb of new life. As the formula used on Ash Wednesday says: "Turn away from sin and hear the good news." In light of the resurrection all of us sinners (or underdogs) can become champions.

PROPHETS: SYMBOLS OF THE "NAKED" TRUTH

Once upon a time (so the story goes), in a far off kingdom there lived an emperor who was full of himself. This emperor became convinced that he needed a new suit of clothes befitting his position. Two unscrupulous tailors promised to make him an unforgettable, extraordinary outfit out of a new material. Only the smartest and wisest people would be able to see it.

At the emperor's final fitting, the tailors pretended to hold up the new outfit. Not wanting to appear stupid, the emperor replied, "Lovely! You've done an excellent job." He asked his attendants who quickly agreed. Later the whole city turned out to see the emperor's new clothes. All were taken aback when they saw him. "Isn't he naked?" they thought. But none would say it out loud for fear of looking foolish. Finally, a boy came to the parade route and asked: "Why doesn't the emperor have any clothes on?"

Recognizing Our Nakedness

Like the little boy in the classic children's story, *The Emperor's New Clothes*, the prophets of the Hebrew Scriptures called upon Israel to recognize her nakedness. Being the conscience of the nation, they condemned Israel for wearing garments of greed and challenged her to put on the cloak of justice.

Prophets were a far cry from the way we often picture them—strangely dressed people who gazed into crystal balls predicting the future. What they were concerned with was the present and how faithfully Israel was living out its covenant with God. As messengers for God, prophets voiced the hard truth of what would happen to Israel if she continued in her selfish, materialistic, and militaristic ways: slavery, destruction, and despair. For example, the prophet Hosea married a prostitute in an attempt to show

Israel her infidelity to the steadfast love of God. Nobody, however, likes to be shown their idols.

Deep concern for the poor and marginalized made the prophets thorns in the sides of Israel's kings. Their words of criticism were seen as a double-edged sword—comforting to some, disturbing to others. In times of war, the words of Micah calling them "to beat our swords into ploughshares" (4:3) were very unsettling. A saying often attributed to the prophets' mission was that they came "to afflict the comfortable and comfort the afflicted." Not the way to win friends in high places.

Our Own Prophets

Some of the prophets' names are familiar to us, e.g., Jeremiah, Isaiah, and Elijah; while others may sound foreign, e.g., Elisha, Zephaniah, and Habakkuk. We remember our own recent prophets: Mother Teresa of Calcutta, Dorothy Day, Pope John XXIII, and Martin Luther King, Jr. In light of our nation's and the world's problems, they call us to be headlights rather than taillights. They challenge us to become thermostats (to transform society) instead of remaining thermometers (to read and follow society). Whatever their day and time, all prophets hunger for righteousness.

During the Easter season, the season of new life, we reflect more seriously on our baptismal call to be Jesus' disciples. Discipleship, whatever the season, invites us to be not only priests and kings but also prophets.

QUESTIONS FOR REVIEW AND REFLECTION

- What are some symbols that have meaning for us and today's young people? What do they communicate, stand for?

- What are some symbols of unconditional love in our time?

- Take a character or event from the Book of Exodus and compare it to your life. Who or what is my Pharaoh? Who is my Moses? Have I had a burning bush experience?

- As with David, how has God worked through a failing or weakness of yours?

- Prophets just weren't persons who lived in the past. Who are some prophets in our midst today? What hard truths are they trying to tell us? Are we listening?

ACTIVITIES

- With older children, ask them to retell the story of Noah's Ark using events and symbols in their lives. For example, they might talk about the devastation caused by an actual, recent flood or tornado or storm. Which objects or actions were symbols of the devastation? Which objects or actions were symbols of hope and love?

- Reconciliation Letter: Have the children put themselves in Jacob's shoes. Invite them to write a letter to Esau sharing their thoughts and emotions over the breakup of their relationship. When finished, ask them whom they really need to write a letter of reconciliation to.

PRAYER STARTER

Invite Abraham into your midst. Allow him to share his journey of faith (Genesis 12) with you. Now share your journey of faith with him—your call, times that you felt close to or far from God, and so on.

CHAPTER 4

Saints as Symbolic Persons

SAINT VINCENT DE PAUL: SYMBOL OF SERVICE TO THE POOR

Saints—they are our patrons and protectors, always ready to receive our petitions and prayers. By their actions they become images, or icons, of God's image, Jesus Christ, and invite us into relationship with him.

One such saint or holy person is Saint Vincent de Paul. He was born of a humble family in France in 1850. His parents wanted their son to receive a good education and raise their standing in society. He happily went along with the idea. In Vincent's time, priesthood was one way of escaping the hard life of a peasant farmer. He took to his studies and quickly advanced, gaining knowledge and prestige.

Vincent's Conversion

Soon he was a mover and shaker among the Parisian elite. His social standing and ambition reached its height when he found work as a tutor and chaplain to the Gondi family, one of the wealthiest families in France.

Yet, a chance encounter with a poor peasant changed all this. When the poor man remarked that he might have died in a state of mortal sin had his confession not been heard, Vincent awoke to the realization that he needed to serve the spiritual and physical needs of the poor.

He soon began tapping his wealthy friends and contacts to help him on behalf of his efforts to help the poor. One such person was Saint Louise de Marillac, whom he served as spiritual director. Together with her, he founded the Sisters of Charity. Vincent said of the Sisters: "Their convent is the sickroom, their chapel the parish, their cloister the streets of the city."

His Ministry

Alongside the Sisters he founded a religious order of men, known as the Vincentians, who focused on missionary work to the poor and clergy education. Vincent's work over the years included aid to imprisoned galley slaves in the ports of Paris. Galley slaves were the people condemned to the backbreaking labor of rowing the boats over the oceans. So great was Vincent's love for these people that one time, it is said, he took over the oars for a man so he could visit his family.

According to legend, his ministry to them might also have been motivated by his experience as the captive of pirates for several years. Whether that story was fact or fiction, his service to the poor is reflected in one of his sayings: "When you leave your prayer to care for a sick person, you leave God for God. To care for a sick person is to pray."

Saint Vincent suffered from ill health in his later years. He died in 1660. He was canonized in 1737, and in 1885, Pope Leo XIII named him the patron of charitable societies. He is often pictured surrounded by poor children. He is also one of the patron saints of hospitals, hospital workers, lepers, and prisons. His feast day is September 27. In 1883, Blessed Frederic Ozanam founded a group devoted to the poor and named it the St. Vincent de Paul Society, in honor of the saint.

It's good to remind ourselves that we may have a few saints-in-the-making in our midst (whatever their disposition may be). Vincent himself was said to be "by nature very subject to anger" and yet he became mild and compassionate.

SAINT THÉRÈSE OF LISIEUX: SYMBOL OF THE "LITTLE WAY"

When most people think of saints, images of martyrdom (stonings, burnings at the stake, public beheadings) and/or acts of great self-denial (selling all of one's property, going far away to proclaim the gospel) fill their minds. Thérèse of Lisieux runs contrary to this idea of sanctity. For her the path to sainthood would be found in the most ordinary and simplest of ways.

Born in Alençon, France in 1873, Thérèse was the youngest of five daughters. Tragedy struck the family, though, when the girls' mother died. With her father working to support the family, Thérèse was left in the care of her older sisters. It felt like another death in the family when her favorite sister, Pauline, joined the local Carmelite monastery when Thérèse was around ten.

The Carmelite

At the age of fourteen Thérèse wished to join the monastery but was first refused by the mother superior and later by the bishop due to her young age. Not accepting defeat, she went to Rome on a pilgrimage. There she appealed to the pope. He told her to trust God's will. Several months later Thérèse was allowed to join the Carmelite monastery where two of her sisters lived.

There she began and lived her religious life, fulfilling her duties—praying, cleaning, cooking, gardening, and laundering—to the best of her ability and with fervent love. Having undergone tremendous suffering over the years, Thérèse died of tuberculosis at the age of twenty-four in 1897. Little would be known of her were it not for the discovery and publication in 1898 of her spiritual autobiography, *The Story of a Soul*.

In this small book, written at the request of her superior-sister, the world would soon discover Thérèse's way—the "little way" as she called it. A name often attributed to her—"the Little Flower"—communicates this idea well. Thérèse saw herself as Jesus' overlooked, forgotten, ordinary wildflower. This did not lead to despair, however, for she knew God was watching her do "little things with great love." Her "little way" was her path to holiness.

Maybe this is why she struck such a chord with and appealed to so many people. Thérèse's life spent hidden behind cloister walls—like so many people's lives spent in the obscurity of the fields, shops, and kitchens—proved that holiness was possible for everyone. In *The Story of a Soul*, she wrote that Christ was most often present to her not "during my hours of prayer…but rather in the midst of my daily occupations."

The Missionary

Thérèse's cause for sainthood proceeded quickly, and she was canonized in 1925. Her feast day is October 1. In the beginning of her vocation, Thérèse had a desire to be a missionary, but her fragile health kept her close to home. This did not prevent her from remembering missionaries, however. Her prayers and letters to them took her far afield. With this in mind, in 1927 she was declared patron saint of missions along with St. Francis Xavier. Further complementing Thérèse's standing in the Church, Pope John Paul II declared her a Doctor of the Church (one of three women) in 1997.

Just as routine and ordinariness filled Thérèse's life, so too does it fill ours. Rather than let it be an obstacle to holiness, though, it might just be our path. Thérèse's "little way" might be "our way" to sanctity us as well, if we do everything with love for God.

SAINT JUAN DIEGO: SYMBOL OF GOD'S LOVE FOR THE DOWNTRODDEN

By 1521 the Spanish conquest of Mexico was complete. The native Aztec culture had been destroyed. They were a defeated people. In addition to a new political system, the Spanish also brought a new religion—Christianity. It was introduced, however, in a strange language, by a foreign people, and, sometimes, under the cruelest of conditions. As a result, very few Aztecs converted to Christianity.

But all that was about to change.

On his way to Mass one December morning in 1531, as he reached the top of a hill, the Aztec convert Juan Diego heard a voice. A woman speaking his native tongue and dressed as an Aztec princess called out his name, "Juanito." She told him that she was "the ever virgin, Holy Mary, Mother of the True God." The Lady instructed Juan Diego to go to the local Spanish bishop and ask that a temple be built on the site—Tepeyac, a former Aztec religious shrine.

"I Am a Nobody"

When he reached the bishop's residence, Juan Diego asked to see him. The bishop listened to his story with skepticism and dismissed it as an old man's active imagination.

Returning to the hill later that evening, Juan Diego encountered the Lady again. He told of his unsuccessful visit to the bishop. Juan Diego then asked that her message be given to someone of "importance, well known, respected, and esteemed, so that they may believe in him; because I am a nobody, I am a small rope, a tiny ladder...." Thankfully, the Lady refused.

Visiting the bishop the next day, Juan Diego was told to bring proof of his encounter with the Lady. When he told her of the request, she promised to fulfill it. Juan Diego was unable to meet the Lady, however. He had to tend to the needs of his dying uncle. He actually tried to avoid her and took another way around the hill. The Lady intercepted him, though, and told Juan Diego not to worry about his uncle because he would be healed.

She then instructed Juan Diego to go to the top of the hill. Given the time of year and the desert terrain, he was not prepared for what he saw—countless roses blooming in December. Returning to the Lady, she arranged them in his *tilma*, a cloth-like fiber garment that served as his coat. With this sign, Juan Diego was prepared to face the bishop.

The Miraculous Image

After enduring another long wait, Juan finally met with the bishop. What captured the bishop's attention weren't the roses blooming unseasonably, but the image that remained on Juan's tilma, the image of the Virgin Mary.

The bishop then believed Juan Diego and agreed to build a temple. Now, some 475 years later, the Basilica of Our Lady of Guadalupe stands at Tepeyac (near present-day Mexico City). In it the tilma of Juan Diego is still preserved.

Juan Diego was canonized by Pope John Paul II on July 31, 2002. His feast day is December 9. Our Lady of

Guadalupe is celebrated December 12. She has also been named the Patroness of the Americas.

Through Saint Juan Diego and Our Lady of Guadalupe, we proclaim that God "visits" us in our language, dress, culture, and, indeed, person.

SAINT ELIZABETH ANN SETON: SYMBOL OF GOD'S CHARITY

When people first think of places where saints lived, the Holy Land, Europe, Latin America all come to mind. Rarely do we think of the United States. This probably has more to do with the relative "newness" of our nation than a lack of holiness on the part of the faithful. Whatever the case, Elizabeth Ann Seton is one of the saints who has changed this situation. She has the distinct title of being the first American-born person to be canonized.

Daughter of New York

Elizabeth was born in New York City in 1774, a few months after the Boston Tea Party, right before the Revolutionary War began. She was brought up in a wealthy Episcopalian home. Through her father, who was a doctor, she learned the virtue of service to others. Unfortunately, tragedy would strike early for Elizabeth, when at the age of three her mother died. What sustained Elizabeth through all the events in her life was her devotion to reading the Scriptures.

In 1794, at the age of twenty, she married William Magee Seton, a wealthy businessman. Over the course of nine happy years together, they had five children. Life, it appeared, couldn't get any better. In addition to the demands of being a wife and mother, Elizabeth and her sister-in-law became concerned about the material conditions of the poor. This led to the formation in 1797 of the Society for the Relief of Poor Widows with Children. Together, the women became known as the "Protestant Sisters of Charity."

Elizabeth's life would soon change, however. Her husband's business went bankrupt, and his health began to deteriorate rapidly. A trip to visit friends in Italy was suggested to improve his well-being. Sadly, William died of tuberculosis shortly after reaching the home of his friends. Through these same friends, however, Elizabeth first discovered the beauty of Catholicism. She was particularly drawn to the Blessed Sacrament.

Mother of a Vast Family

Upon her return home to New York in 1805, after a profound inner struggle, Elizabeth became a Catholic. Not unexpectedly, her relatives disapproved, and she soon found herself without any financial support. After a failed attempt at starting a boarding school in New York, in 1808 a priest invited her to establish a school for girls in Baltimore. From these humble beginnings, Elizabeth Seton is credited with founding the Catholic parochial system in America.

From the small group of women who joined Elizabeth to teach would come the Sisters of Charity, the first congregation of women religious founded in the United States. During Elizabeth's lifetime twenty communities would be established. Her legacy today is impressive: six religious congregations with close to 5,000 members, plus hundreds of social service centers and hospitals throughout the United States and the world. All this sprang from Elizabeth's love for Jesus and her sisters and brothers in God's family.

Plagued by tuberculosis, Elizabeth, now known as Mother Seton, died in Emmitsburg on January 4, 1821.

The National Shrine of St. Elizabeth Ann Seton is located there. She was canonized by Pope Paul VI on September 14, 1975. The pope said, "She is the first daughter of the United States of America to be glorified with this incomparable attribute." Her feast day is January 4.

SAINT BRIGID: SYMBOL OF GENEROSITY

The two are almost synonymous today—Ireland and Catholic. This was not always the case, however. In Brigid's day paganism still held the hearts of many Irish. In no small way, Brigid would change this and win countless persons for Christ.

Though the exact year of her birth is uncertain (sometime in the late fifth century, which made her a contemporary of St. Patrick), her societal standing is not. Brigid was the product of a clash between two worlds, the result of a union between her mother, Brocessa, a slave, and her father, Dubtach, a pagan chieftain. Privilege was not to be hers, though. Prior to her birth, her mother was sold to another man on the condition that Brigid would return when she was old enough to work for her father. While she was with her mother, Brigid was baptized and taught the basics of the Christian faith.

Brigid's Generosity

Eventually, Brigid became a servant in her father's house. Dubtach would soon find this to be an exercise in frustration because of Brigid's generosity. In her presence no one left hungry or penniless.

One day Dubtach took Brigid to the castle of the king. While he was inside, a leper passed by the chariot with Brigid waiting. Moved at the sight of him, the girl was sad that there was nothing to give him. Then she took her father's jeweled sword, and gave it to the leper. When Dubtach returned to the chariot, he was beside himself. In anger he wanted to punish her. However, the king, who was a Christian, stopped him. He was so impressed by her gesture that he encouraged Brigid's father to free her, which he did.

Shortly after that Brigid visited her mother, who worked at a dairy farm. Because her mother was frail and overworked, Brigid took her mother's place in tending the farm. The owner was moved by the girl's work and wanted to reward her. Rather than asking for any material thing, Brigid asked for and was given her mother's freedom.

A Bride of Christ

When Brigid returned to her father's house, she found that he was arranging her marriage. She tested her father's patience again by declaring that she wished to become a bride and virgin for Christ. At first he refused his permission, but he soon relented. Together with seven other women Brigid took religious vows and established a community at Kildare, "the place of the oak." Brigid would use this place to lead people to Christ. Here we find the Christian theme of movement, of conversion. Inviting people to conversion was at the center of her life.

Her reputation as an abbess quickly grew. Kildare, which now had both male and female communities, became a center of learning. From there Brigid traveled on chariot throughout Ireland, founding new monasteries. The people held her in such esteem that they gave her the title of "Mary of the Gael."

St. Brigid's feast day, the day on which she died in 525 AD, is February 1. She is the patron of sailors, students, and dairy workers.

SAINT PATRICK: SYMBOL OF NEW LIFE IN CHRIST

When I read and hear of stories about Saint Patrick my thoughts quickly drift to snakes, shamrocks, parades, and green beer. As I have discovered, though, in addition to the various legends attributed to him and the popular cultural celebrations of him, Patrick's is an amazing story of discipleship in Christ.

Like his counterpart, Saint Brigid, the exact years of his birth and death are uncertain. (The general dates given by many are from 385–461 AD.) Born in Britain (probably somewhere in present-day Scotland), Patrick was the son of a Roman public official. His family was Christian. In fact, his father was a deacon. His grandfather had been a priest. Patrick, however, was far from saintly.

Patrick Turns to Prayer

Patrick's comfortable life took a dramatic turn when, at the age of the sixteen, he was captured by Irish raiders. Unable to escape, he was taken to Ireland as a slave. There he was sold to a local chieftain and worked for six years herding sheep.

The time was not a total loss, however. The desolate mountains of Ireland and the solitary life of a herdsman enabled Patrick to spend long hours in prayer. Rather than destroy his faith, this experience actually strengthened it. What he saw as punishment for laxity in faith became the training grounds for a future missionary. While in Ireland, Patrick learned the native Celtic language. He would eventually use it to lead the Irish people to faith in Jesus Christ.

Escape was never far from his mind, though. When the opportunity presented itself, he seized it. After an arduous journey of some 200 miles to the sea, he found a boat to take him back home. While there he tried to make sense of all that had happened, knowing deep within himself that it had not been in vain. Traveling to Gaul (present-day France) Patrick studied for the priesthood and was ordained. A sense of restlessness remained, however. Resolution eventually came in the form of a vision. A person whom he knew from his days in Ireland appeared to him in a dream and gave him a message: "Come back and walk among us once more."

Rather than return angry and bitter to his former oppressors, Patrick went carrying the light of the Resurrection. His life was evidence that the life, death, and resurrection of Jesus can conquer the greatest of transgressions. Reconciliation can be won. Establishing himself in Armagh, Patrick began a life (close to thirty years) of Christian missionary witness to the pagan people of Ireland. In the process he established countless churches and monasteries, organized dioceses throughout the land, all the while literally baptizing thousands of people.

Naturally, because of this legacy he has been named the patron saint of the emerald isle. Saint Patrick's feast day is celebrated March 17, the day on which he died.

SAINT CATHERINE OF SIENA: SYMBOL OF MYSTICISM

Unlike so many people, saints defy the expectations of their times. Catherine of Siena is no exception. Born in 1347, Catherine was the twenty-fourth out of twenty-five children (her mother's name was Lapa which means "fruitful bee"). At the age of six, Catherine had the first of many mystical experiences. Jesus appeared to her, surrounded by Saints Peter, Paul, and John the Evangelist. Catherine's spiritual connection with Jesus would only grow stronger over the years. At the age of seven, she made a solemn vow of virginity.

Engaged to Jesus

Thinking that Catherine's strong religious leanings just a passing fancy, her parents arranged for her to marry. When Catherine resisted their plans, they basically made her a servant of the family. At age fifteen, rather than be married, she defied the wishes of her family and cut off her beautiful hair. Eventually convinced of Catherine's commitment, her father allowed her to join the Third Order of Dominicans.

For close to three years, Catherine remained in a small room in her parents' house. Her time was spent in prayer and severe fasting, basically secluded from the world. Here during a mystical encounter, she was visited by Jesus. Catherine was betrothed to him, and Jesus placed a ring, visible only to her, on her finger.

Shortly thereafter, Catherine emerged from her self-imposed confinement and began to attend to the needs of Siena's sick and poor, and, in 1374, victims of the plague. (For this she would later be named a patron of nursing.) Catherine soon attracted the attention of others. A group of followers developed who aided her in ministry. Others, however, resented her growing reputation, especially because she was a laywoman with no formal education.

CAPTIVE POPES?

After another mystical experience, Catherine felt called to address issues of Church-wide concern, and she became a public figure. The biggest issue besetting the Church at this time was the papacy's continued residence in Avignon

(1309–1378). Popes had resided in this French city for a whole host of political reasons. Whether or not it was true, their presence gave the impression that the papacy was under the influence of the king of France.

In the summer of 1376, Catherine traveled to Avignon to encourage Pope Gregory XI to return to Rome. In one of her letters she wrote: "No longer resist the will of God, for the starving sheep wait for you to return to the see of St. Peter." Fortified by Catherine's appeals, Gregory XI returned to Rome, but soon died. Though now back in Rome, the papacy would face a new threat—the Great Western Schism (1378–1417).

Catherine the Peacemaker

After Gregory's death, because of deep divisions in the Church there were two, and later three, claimants to the office of pope. Just as the spirit gave new life to the infant church on Pentecost, Catherine sought to bring a spirit of reconciliation to the divisions of her time as well. Exhausted by her efforts for unity, Catherine died in 1380 at the age of thirty-three. Before she died, Catherine received the stigmata (the wounds of Jesus), visible only to herself.

Saint Catherine wrote one of the greatest works of mystical theology, *The Dialogue*. Her biography by Raymond of Capua, Catherine's spiritual director, added to her popularity and appeal. She was canonized in 1461. Her feast day is April 29. Along with Saint Francis of Assisi, Catherine is patron of Italy.

As testament to her lasting significance in the Church, Pope Paul VI declared Saint Catherine a Doctor of the Church (one of three women so named) on October 4, 1970.

QUESTIONS FOR REVIEW AND REFLECTION

- We are constantly looking for heroes and role models today. Why or why not do we consider such figures saints?

- If Saint Patrick entrusted his missionary vocation to you, where would you go to proclaim the good news of Jesus Christ? Why? How do you think you would be received?

- Saint Catherine of Siena was not afraid to speak the truth, even to the pope. She wrote him letters expressing how she felt on a variety of topics. You're invited to write a "letter" to the pope. What questions are on your mind? What do you want to say to him?

ACTIVITIES

- This can be done as a class or individually. Using markers, crayons, or colored paper, have your children make a flower surrounded by petals. On each petal they can write one thing they can do to share the love of God with others in simple everyday activities like Saint Thérèse of Lisieux.

- Like the saints, be a model of charity and justice. Volunteer as an individual or class in your family, parish, school, or wider community.

PRAYER STARTER

The saints held their faith in many hostile and pagan environments. We too live in a society where "false gods" are worshipped. In our desire for a deeper relationship with Jesus, what are some things—false gods—that get in the way?

CHAPTER 5

Saints as Symbols of Virtue

SAINT ANDREW KIM TAEGON: SYMBOL OF FAITH

Virtue. We don't hear this word often today. But the need for people of strong character and principle, for people who have good habits, has never gone away. The Christian tradition offers the saints, holy men and women of God, as models of virtue. As exemplars in putting their faith into action, the saints show us that our actions reflect who we are.

Of the three theological virtues, named because they have "their origin, motive, and object" (*Catechism of the Catholic Church*, #1812) in God, faith is listed first. The Letter to the Hebrews states, "Faith is the realization of what is hoped for and evidence of things not seen" (11:1). Ultimately, faith—relationship with God—is gift. The challenge is for us to accept this invitation. One person who professed, witnessed and spread the Catholic faith was Saint Andrew Kim Taegon of Korea.

The Blood of Martyrs
Because no foreign priests had been allowed to stay in Korea,

lay people in the late 18th century began the Catholic community there. The community was small and in need of priests to celebrate the sacraments. Catholics there would soon face persecution and martyrdom, including Andrew Kim's own father and grandfather.

Andrew Kim was born of nobility on August 21, 1821, in Korea After his baptism at age fifteen (1836), Andrew Kim responded to God's call and the needs of his people. He traveled some 1,300 miles to begin seminary studies in Macao, China. In 1845, he was ordained a priest in Shanghai. In so doing he became the first native-born Korean priest. After several unsuccessful attempts, Andrew Kim, along with two other French priests, returned to his native Korea.

In 1846, while arranging for more missionaries to enter, he was arrested and imprisoned. Rather than see this as a defeat for his ministry, Andrew Kim wrote to the Catholic community, exhorting them to not lose heart, to keep following Jesus, and to continue in the way of the saints.

Tortured and beheaded, Andrew Kim was martyred outside Seoul on September 16, 1846. Along with 102 other Korean martyrs, he was canonized on May 6, 1984, by Pope John Paul II. Unlike other canonizations, which have been held at the Vatican, this one took place in Andrew Kim's homeland of Korea. There the pope said, "The death of the martyrs is similar to the death of Christ on the Cross, because, like his, theirs has become the beginning of new life." The feast day of Andrew Kim and his companions is September 20.

The Seeds of Faith

It is hard to believe, but in its first hundred years the Catholic Church in Korea faced ongoing persecution with over 10,000 faithful believers losing their lives. Like the ancient adage says, however, the blood of the martyrs became the seeds of a dynamic faith community today.

As teachers and parents we are given the privilege and daunting opportunity of inviting those under our guidance into a deeper relationship with God, with all the excitement and anxiety that it brings. This is no easy task in a wounded and cynical world. The apostles' request to Jesus, "Increase our faith" (Luke 17:5), seems to grow louder in our hearts.

Probably few, if any, of us will be called upon to die for our faith in the same way Andrew Kim and his companions did. Yet, sometimes we may feel overwhelmed, even underappreciated, at the responsibility of being parents and teachers, witnesses to Christ. Faith tells us, though, that we are where we're supposed to be. God reaches out to us in friendship so we can do likewise with those in our care. God invites all of us to live—not with the faith we have in ourselves but with the faith that God has in each of us. Look out mountains!

SAINT TERESA OF ÁVILA: SYMBOL OF HOPE

"I hope I do well on this test," one of my students said.

"Did you study?" I asked. "Nope," he replied. "Well that's not hope. That's wishful thinking," I responded.

How often we confuse the active, participatory, and dedicated theological virtue of hope—a deep and abiding trust in God's providence—with a passive, noninvolved, and irresponsible popular understanding of it. Jesus was hopeful about the coming kingdom of God. He actively sought to bring it forth. Likewise, as disciples, we are called to be hopeful co-creators with Jesus in constructing and building up the kingdom of God.

One person who acted on Jesus' invitation to build God's kingdom was Teresa of Ávila. Hope was a virtue she would call upon and exercise throughout her life.

Teresa's Vocation and Illness

Teresa was born in Ávila, Spain, on March 28, 1515. Her comfortable life was upset at the age of fifteen, when her mother died. At this point her father entrusted her care and education to a convent of Augustinian women, a common practice at that time. When she returned home several years later, Teresa felt called to the religious life.

In 1535, at the age of twenty and against her father's wishes, Teresa joined the local Carmelite convent. Illness was to plague her stay there. As a result, a year later her father had to take her home. There her health continued to deteriorate. At one point she fell into a coma and came close to death. For almost three years she remained paralyzed from the waist down.

Eventually Teresa recovered and returned to the convent. This brought little consolation, however. As was the case at many religious communities, life there was not challenging. Little was asked of her. This all changed, when at the age of thirty-nine, Teresa experienced a mystical vision of the "sorely wounded Christ." From it, she felt called to reform her own, lax spiritual life. In the end, she formed a new Carmelite community in Ávila in 1562.

Reformer, Mystic, and Writer

Unlike her life in the convent she had just left, Teresa and her sisters lived very simply, admitted few visitors, and spent most of their time studying and praying. Symbolic of their austere way of life was their name—the Discalced (literally "shoeless") Carmelites. God blessed Teresa with special spiritual insights and grace.

However, her new foundation was met with suspicion and opposition from the townspeople and Church leaders. Despite this, she went on to found sixteen other convents.

In addition to her work as a reformer, Teresa was also a spiritual writer. Perhaps her greatest and most influential work is *The Interior Castle*, written in 1577. In it Teresa compared a person's relationship with God to a beautiful castle, with Jesus at the center. The castle has a series of rooms, which represent different stages of prayer and spiritual growth.

Throughout it all—physical sickness, public opposition, and little material comfort—Teresa never lost her sense of humor. This is best evidenced when, after she had been thrown from her carriage, she remarked to God: "If this is how you treat your friends, it is no wonder you have so few."

Shortly after founding her last convent, Teresa returned to Ávila in poor health. The trip was too much for her, and she died several days later in October 1582. Canonized by Pope Gregory XV in 1622, her feast day is October 15. Testifying to the esteem that the Church had long held regarding her, Pope Paul VI declared her a Doctor of the Church (along with Saint Catherine of Siena) on September 27, 1970. Teresa and Catherine were the first women to be so honored.

As a reformer, mystic, and writer, Teresa is an outstanding example of the virtue of hope.

BLESSED MIGUEL PRO: SYMBOL OF LOVE

"So faith, hope, love remain, these three; but the greatest of these of is love" (1 Corinthians 13:13)

As important as the first two theological virtues are, Saint Paul declares that love (also referred to charity) is the foundational one. The *Catechism of the Catholic Church* states that "charity [love] is the theological virtue by which we love God above all things for his own sake, and our neighbor as ourselves for the love of God" (1822). Saint Thomas Aquinas says that "to love someone is to will the good of another." The ultimate sign of willing the good of another is found in the incarnation of God's son, which we prepare for every Advent season and celebrate during Christmas. As Saint John's Gospel says: "God so loved the world that he gave his only son" (3:16).

It goes without saying that all saints, in one form or another, manifest the virtue of love. Blessed Miguel Pro was an example of love under the most trying of circumstances. Born in Mexico on January 13, 1891, to a devout Catholic family, Miguel entered the Society of Jesus (popularly known as the Jesuits) at the age of twenty in 1911.

Due to rising anti-Catholicism in Mexico, he was forced to continue his priestly training in California, and later in Spain. He was ordained a priest in Belgium in 1925.

After prayerful consideration, Miguel asked for and was granted permission to return to Mexico. The religious persecution had become worse there. Churches were closed or destroyed. Celebrations of the Mass and the other sacraments were forbidden. Priests went into hiding or left the country for fear for their lives. Because of this, an underground church had developed.

Underground Priest

Miguel was well aware of the danger he was placing himself in, including death, when he ministered to the spiritual needs of the Mexican faithful. He carried out his ministry secretly, undercover, to avoid being captured. He celebrated Mass, baptisms, marriages, and confessions in individual homes or other hiding places so as to avoid detection. He also was also able to establish a network so people who needed food and other necessities were provided for.

A master of disguise, Father Pro carried out his ministry dressed like a street sweeper, beggar, chauffeur, and mechanic. He did whatever was necessary to help his people keep the faith when all appeared lost. One story tells of him returning to a house where he narrowly escaped capture. He came back dressed as a policeman. With his usual bravado and sense of humor he demanded to know from his fellow officers why they hadn't caught Pro yet!

Viva Cristo Rey

Though it lasted nearly a year, Miguel's ministry would soon come to an end. After being falsely implicated in an assassination attempt on an influential Mexican politician, he was a marked man. Eventually, his hiding place was betrayed and he was captured. There was no trial. The government made an example of Fr. Pro and warned people not to defy its authority. Fr. Pro was sentenced to death.

On November 23, 1927, Miguel was taken before a firing squad. The President of Mexico had invited journalists and other military personnel to watch. When Fr. Pro was asked if he had any last request, he said that he would like a few moments to pray. Stretching out his arms in the shape of the cross, as the firing squad took aim, Miguel firmly said: "Viva Cristo Rey" ("Long live Christ the King"). Shortly thereafter he was shot to death.

Though forbidden to have a public Mass, throngs of people gathered to see Fr. Pro buried. His remains are interred at his shrine in Mexico City. Pope John Paul II declared him "blessed" on September 25, 1988. His feast day is November 23.

SAINT ANGELA MERICI: SYMBOL OF PRUDENCE

The virtues of prudence, fortitude, justice, and temperance bear the name "cardinal" because they act like a hinge does to keep a door centered and balanced (*cardo* means "hinge.")

The first of these virtues, prudence, might at first make young people think of something to flee from or tense up at (think "prude"). Yet, practical judgment, or prudence, is a mark all should strive to attain. The Book of Proverbs says, "The prudent man looks where he is going" (14:15). The ability to look things over and choose the best course of action is a life skill that we must all work toward. One person who exercised prudence, who made the right decisions at the right time, was Saint Angela Merici.

Angela was born in Desenzano, a small town in Northern Italy on March 21, 1474. Not unlike many children of her day, Angela was left an orphan at the age of ten. She and her older sister went to live with an uncle in a town nearby. Sadly, her sister died too. In the midst of such sorrow, Angela had a consoling vision: Her sister was in heaven. Shortly thereafter, at age of fifteen, Angela became a Franciscan tertiary.

When Angela was twenty her uncle died, and she returned to her hometown. Distressed by the conditions of her times, she began to catechize the poor children in town. During this time she had another vision, which revealed that one day she would establish a community of women dedicated to the care and education of the poor, especially young women. Angela's school was quickly successful, and she was invited to begin another at the nearby town of Brescia.

Angela was struck blind while on a trip to the Holy Land. Rather than return home, she continued on her pilgrimage. On it, unable to see, she practiced a devotion of the heart rather than sight. On her way, though, while praying before a crucifix, her sight returned. The following year she had an audience with the pope. So strong was her commitment to the education of children, that when Pope Clement VII asked her to take over a community of women religious serving as nurses, she refused.

Eventually, in 1535, Angela and a group of like-minded women formed the Company of Saint Ursula (often called the Ursuline sisters today). Its mission was to teach religion (which later expanded to all subjects) to poor children. Though we take it for granted today, Angela's community of women is said to be the first group of women religious to serve beyond the cloister as well as the first teaching order of women.

Her feast day, which is the day on which she died in 1540, is January 27. Pope Pius VII canonized her in 1807.

Whether as a parent or educator, her words ring as true today as they did in her day: "If according to times and needs you should be obliged to make fresh rules and change current things, do it with prudence and good advice."

SAINT JEROME EMILIANI: SYMBOL OF COURAGE

If ever an age called for courage—the assurance of firmness in difficulties and constancy in the pursuit of the good (*Catechism of the Catholic Church*, #1808)—it is our own. This cry for people of courage, however, has been echoed down through the centuries as well. One place where we can look for models of courage is the saints. In them we need not look far to discover a group of people who took action, stood up for what was right, and did things others were unwilling to do. A great model of courage, sometimes called fortitude, is Saint Jerome Emiliani.

Jerome, the youngest of four brothers, was born in the Italian city-state of Venice in 1481. He was playful and adventurous as a young child but was heartbroken by his father's death when Jerome was in his early teens. After that, he was angry and alone.

Giving his life some direction, Jerome joined the Venetian army in 1506. An able soldier, he soon found himself commanding a castle fortress in northern Italy. In 1508, while defending the fortress, Jerome's troops were defeated. He was captured and imprisoned in a dungeon.

During his imprisonment, Jerome had a spiritual awakening. The battlefield lost its allure, and he found himself drawn to the message and person of Jesus the Christ. At some point, he was able to free himself from his chains. Fulfilling a vow, Jerome made a pilgrimage to the shrine of Our Lady of Treviso, where, in gratitude for his freedom, he placed there the chains that had once shackled him. The people there held him in such high regard that they appointed him mayor. This was not to last, however.

Priestly Ministry

When he returned home to Venice, he began studies for the priesthood. In the midst of his preparations, he couldn't help but notice how Venice had been devastated by war. Lives had been destroyed, disease was rampant, food and water were difficult to secure, and, to top it all off, there were scores of young children who had lost their parents. Following his ordination in 1518, he felt a particular call, maybe due to the loss of his father at such a young age, to respond to the plight of orphans.

Using his own money and house in the beginning, he cared for as many orphans' physical and spiritual needs as possible. Eventually, Jerome was asked to establish orphanages for children throughout northern Italy. Additionally, he also was given care of a hospital and founded a shelter for repentant prostitutes.

Steadily, Jerome drew followers to himself. In 1532, the Company of the Servants of the Poor (Somascan Fathers and Brothers) was formed, whose mission was to help needy youth. Having fallen ill caring for the sick, Jerome died of the plague on February 8, 1537. This is the day his feast is celebrated. He was canonized on July 16, 1767, by Pope Clement XIII. In 1928, as testament to his ministry, Pope Pius XI named Jerome the patron of orphans and abandoned children.

How much courage it must have taken for Jerome to put down his weapons and fight for Christ. Likewise, as believers we are called upon each day to courageously speak the truth of Christianity to a culture that oftentimes would rather close its ears. It is in this spirit that we say; "Saint Jerome Emiliani, pray for us."

SAINT KATHARINE DREXEL: SYMBOL OF JUSTICE

Our world is one of extreme inequalities: some people's closets are full of designer labels while others barely have clothes on their backs; some live in mansions while others make do with tin shacks; some eat to a gluttonous degree while others go hungry.

We recognize that things have to change and some of us take steps to enact change. The saints among us strive to become models of justice. One such person was Saint Katharine Drexel. In both word and action, Katharine showed a "constant and firm will to give [her] due to God and neighbor" (*Catechism of the Catholic Church*, #1807).

Katharine was born on November 26, 1858, the daughter of a prominent and wealthy Philadelphia family. Sadly, her mother died weeks after her birth. A year later her father married Emma Bouvier who, due to her generosity and compassion, was known as "the Lady Bountiful of Philadelphia." She would have a profound role in shaping Katharine's sense of justice by demonstrating that wealth was meant to be shared with others.

You would expect a child born into such privilege to be above the cares and concerns of the world. But due to her parents, education, and travels, Katharine was sensitized to the plight of poor. Over time she became especially concerned about Native Americans and African Americans.

Katherine's Turning Point

Unfortunately, in 1881, Katharine's stepmother died and, two years later, her father also died. Along with her two sisters, Katharine inherited fourteen million dollars. She was at a turning point in her life.

One event that proved pivotal was a private meeting Katharine had with Pope Leo XIII. In the course of their conversation, she spoke on behalf of her friend and spiritual advisor, Bishop James O'Connor. Financing many of the bishop's educational and spiritual endeavors out West, she encouraged the pope to send missionaries to help Bishop O'Connor. Katharine was taken aback when the pope said, "Why not become a missionary yourself?"

Over the course of several years, Katharine thought deeply about a call to religious life. In 1891, since no religious order focused on ministry to Native Americans and African Americans, she founded her own community—the Sisters of the Blessed Sacrament for Indians and Colored People. Devoting her life to the spiritual and physical needs of these people, Katharine would spend the rest of her days giving her inheritance away for the cause of justice.

Educating for Justice

Focusing on education, Katharine soon opened schools throughout the West and South. It is all the more impressive that she did this during an age of prejudice and discrimination.

Perhaps Katharine's most notable achievement is Xavier University (New Orleans). Founded in 1925, it is the only predominantly black Catholic institution of higher learning in the United States.

In 1935, Mother Katharine suffered a heart attack and retired from active ministry. The succeeding years would find her promoting and praying for the causes of justice that were so close to her heart—Native Americans and African Americans. Katharine died on March 3, 1955. On October 1, 2000, this champion of justice was declared a saint by Pope John Paul II. Her feast day is March 3.

In our lives as Christians, justice takes center stage. Justice, as it did for Katharine, calls us not only to deal with the effects of poverty, but also with the causes.

VENERABLE MATTHEW TALBOT: SYMBOL OF TEMPERANCE

Whether you use the word *temperance* or the more familiar term *moderation*, I'd be willing to bet that neither of them make the top ten list of favored character traits. The word "temperance" sounds so restrictive. For many, the word they hear next is "don't" or "stop." This does not go over well in our indulgent and excessive culture. Yet there is much to be said for this virtue "that moderates the attraction of pleasures and provides balance in the use of created goods" (*Catechism of the Catholic Church*, #1809).

One person who struggled to live a life of balance was Matthew Talbot. He was born on May 2, 1856, in Dublin,

Ireland. His family was poor. His father, a dockworker, found it hard to make enough income to support the family.

Unlike most children today, Matthew received little schooling and was out working around twelve years of age. Over the years he would labor as a messenger boy, dock-hand, bricklayer, and the like. Unfortunately, through both his family and his work, Matthew was introduced to alcohol at a young age. It had long been a thorn in the side of his family—his father, as well as his brothers (except one), were all alcoholics. Matthew soon began to drink heavily.

Like so many alcoholics, then and now, Matthew's life lost all sense of balance and moderation. Most of his wages were spent on alcohol. When drunk, he became angry and argumentative, which often led to fights. It even reached the point where Matthew sometimes sold some of his possessions or stole from others just so he could drink.

One day he was meeting up with some friends at a nearby pub. Out of money, he thought his friends would buy him some beers. Rather than invite Matthew to join them, they passed by him. It was at this point that Matthew knew he had to stop drinking and take "the pledge."

For the next three months, Matthew, who was around thirty at the time, said that he would not drink. Knowing that he needed support in this commitment, he went to church for confession and received the Eucharist for the first time in years. Three months turned into a lifelong pledge. It shouldn't be assumed, however, that this was easy for him. Matthew struggled on the road to recovery. He would remark to one of his sisters years later: "Never look down on a man who cannot give up the drink. It's easier to get out of hell."

Over the years a real transformation took place. Helping in this process, Matthew began each day with daily Mass as well as practicing other spiritual disciplines such as the rosary and fasting. For him, the Eucharist was a source of great strength. He also became devoted to reading the lives of the saints. Later this would lead to him becoming a Secular Franciscan. Recognizing his past, Matthew attempted to repay his past debts. One way he did was through his financial support of religious organizations.

He once said: "Three things I cannot escape: the eye of God, the voice of conscience, the stroke of death. In company, guard your tongue. In your family, guard your temper. When alone, guard your thoughts."

Matthew Talbot's life ended on May 7, 1925 while he was on his way to Mass. In 1973, Pope Paul VI declared Matthew to be "venerable" which means that the Church sees in him a holiness of life worthy of imitation. So begins his path to possible canonization.

Like Matthew, we are empowered by the Spirit to break the chains of slavery and to walk upright with the Lord. For Matthew his addiction to alcohol held him down, while for others it may be eating too much food or spending too much money on things they simply do not need. Fear and complacency are never the answer. New life in the resurrected Christ is the path to spiritual fullness.

QUESTIONS FOR REVIEW AND REFLECTION

- Saint Jerome Emiliani was an advocate for homeless children. When have you felt like an orphan? Abandoned? Alone? Lacking support and family?

- When have we exercised prudence in our life? What are some obstacles that get in the way of us exercising prudence?

- Saint Katharine Drexel offered herself in service to the

other. In the process she discovered the "Other"—God. When have you discovered God in service to others?

- It is hard to admit but all of us have areas in our lives that are out of balance. Share with one another a way in which your life is out of balance and in need of temperance.

ACTIVITIES

- In the spirit of Saint Teresa of Ávila's writings, invite your learners to draw a castle. On it have them write one area in their life they need to change or in which they need to grow so they can be better disciples of Jesus. Allow them to decorate their castles as well.

- Look at current newspapers and magazines for examples of how prudence is (or is not) being put into practice.

- Imagine for moment that you inherited, like Saint Katharine Drexel, $14 million. How would you use your inheritance? What acts of justice would you engage in?

PRAYER STARTER

Many persons believe that our modern age is characterized by despair, pessimism, and cynicism. How can we restore a sense of hope within ourselves? What is one thing we can do to show our hope in God?

CHAPTER 6

Symbols of the Christian Journey

ENCOUNTERING THE MYSTERY: SYMBOLS OF THE MASS

"People change." Yes, that's what he said. I'd asked my friend to capture what good liturgy should do for us. I find myself in agreement with his simple but powerful words.

It is through the Mass—the symbolic drama of the Paschal Mystery realized—that the Spirit invites us into deeper relationship and discipleship with Jesus the Christ. Three primary symbols are the Assembly, the Word, and the Eucharist.

Assembly: No One Gets Left Behind

If there is one thing that characterizes Catholics, it is our sense of community. In a culture wrapped in individualism, the Catholic tradition says it's not about "me," but about "we." Jesus saves us not as a person, but as a people. The place we see this liturgically made most manifest is in the gathered assembly—the body of Christ.

However, that experience of God mediated in and through the assembly is, for many, more ideal than actual.

How often do we still hear and say that "Father said (or did) Mass." It may sound surprising to Catholic ears but the assembly, with the priest presiding, "celebrates" the Eucharist. How often do we forget that holiness is not just found in the sanctuary, "up on the altar," but in the people seated right next to us? As a result, the Sign of Peace should not be an awkward, formal moment in the liturgy, but an expression of friendship in the Lord preparing us to enter into the eucharistic banquet.

One of the key phrases that emerged from Vatican II (*The Constitution on the Sacred Liturgy*) is "full, active, and conscious participation." Catholics have always been good at recognizing God in the Eucharist (often imaged using the word *vertical*), but we are still waking up to the other mediation of God through community (here the word *horizontal* is used).

Word: Tell Us a Story

People are storytellers. We love stories. In fact, we are the stories we tell. Some people say the reason God created us was because God too loves stories. The Mass is one big story, specifically the story of the life, death, and resurrection of Jesus.

When God's word is proclaimed at Mass, we don't just learn about God; we actually encounter God. We are not hearing about God, but actually meeting God through the revealed word. It is in this sense that we can say that there are "two tables of the Lord"—the ambo and the altar. Foreshadowing the Eucharist that is to come, the word is then broken open in the homily by the priest.

The proclaimed word leads us to the table of the Lord, which nourishes us to go out and become Christ for others.

Eucharist: We Are What We Eat

In the midst of our hectic and busy lives, the Mass gives us time to slow down and say "Thanks." "Thanksgiving" is what the Eucharist is all about. We celebrate our incorporation into Christ's body by eating and drinking his body and blood. No longer does the shadow keep us in darkness, but the light of redemption leads us to wholeness. The bread that we eat, in contrast to our fast food culture, reminds us that what we really hunger for is eternal life. Just as water is necessary for the body, the wine that we drink tells us that we are dependent upon Christ. In a culture that seeks to avoid pain at all cost, the altar that we see says that sacrifice is a part of our lives and can't be avoided. There can be no resurrection without first undergoing crucifixion.

This eucharistic thanksgiving leads us out into the wider community to feed and clothe those who are in need. As the bread and wine are transformed into the body and blood of Jesus, through our partaking of them we must change the world to better reflect Jesus.

SYMBOLS OF THE RITE OF PENANCE: RECONCILIATION AS THE PATH TO LIFE

One thing Pope John Paul II said a lot was "I'm sorry." For numerous sins of the Church—anti-Semitism, crusades, inquisitions, wars of religion, treatment of women, Christian division—he publicly apologized and sought repentance and reconciliation. As hard as it may be for us to recognize and admit our own sins, the Church offers us a similar opportunity for healing through the Sacrament of Reconciliation, or Penance, and its many symbols.

Christ

The most obvious symbol of reconciliation is Jesus Christ. It is in and through his life, death, and resurrection that we are restored to relationship with God the Father. A life of alienation due to sin is turned to one of friendship on the path of discipleship.

As an *alter christus*, or "other Christ," the priest is a primary symbol of the sacrament as well. In his very person, the priest models and offers to the penitent the healing love of Christ. He also serves as the representative of the Church that desires us always to be at table with it joined in praise and celebration.

Form

Though we may take it for granted now, an interesting symbol to emerge from the Second Vatican Council's (1962–1965) liturgical renewal is the *form* of reconciliation itself. There is not one rite for this sacrament, but three: 1) individual confession and absolution; 2) communal gathering of penitents followed by individual confession and absolution; and 3) communal gathering of penitents including general confession and absolution.

The communal experience with individual confession (second rite) is probably the one that most children and young people are familiar with. These liturgies are often held during Lent and Advent. This is for good reason. In a culture marked by excessive individualism, we gather in faith admitting our sinfulness. In this way we communicate that sin not only harms our relationship with God (vertical dimension), but also our relationship with others (horizontal dimension). As a result, the gathered community becomes a symbol of the pilgrim church—a sinful people journeying toward the fullness of God's kingdom.

Place

Depending on one's age the *place* of reconciliation has changed too. Many churches today have what are called reconciliation rooms rather than traditional confessionals. Though beneficial for many people, the physical structure of the confessional can convey a sense that sin is private (between me and the priest). Also, given their often dark and shadowy interiors, the experience of God may not be as full as the sacrament wants to present.

Reconciliation rooms, however, offer the penitent a more personal and complete encounter with the priest confessor (and by extension God). Though this setting allows for anonymous confession, in the face-to-face exchange between the priest and penitent, one is better able to sense and experience the merciful, compassionate, and healing forgiveness of God.

Healing Touch

Touch, as experienced in the imposition of hands, is another powerful symbol. A healing and reconciling touch was central to Jesus' ministry (cf. Matthew 3:2–3; Mark 7:32; Luke 4:40). Through the mediating presence of the priest during the prayer of absolution, penitents can physically feel that Jesus is not aloof and distant, but actually present touching them, inviting them back into communion with him. In a society (and church) that is increasingly fearful of touch, the power of this symbol should not be underestimated.

Words

Finally, the words of this sacrament are also symbolic. The Scriptures proclaimed, the confession of sins, the act of contrition, and the words of absolution, all image for us the loving and forgiving God of Jesus, who came not to condemn us but to save us.

SYMBOLS OF ADVENT: LEARNING TO WAIT

If there is one word we hate to hear in our culture it's "wait." If someone really wants to rub salt in our wounds they'll say, "Patience is a virtue." This is usually met with a less than enthusiastic smile. Despite all of our fast foods, instant messengers, and drive-thrus, we still spend a significant amount of time waiting. Unfortunately, our culture has a very negative attitude toward waiting. If we don't get something quickly, instantaneously, right on time, something is wrong.

So what does the Church do right after Thanksgiving when advertisers are already pushing Christmas? It tells us to wait by inviting us to enter into the season of Advent (Latin for "coming"). In and through Advent we prepare to celebrate Jesus' multiple comings: Christ's incarnation some 2,000 years ago, Christ's presence in our midst today, and Christ's glorious return at the end of time.

One way we help ourselves and others "wait" during Advent is to make use of the season's multiple symbols: the Jesse Tree, the Advent wreath, and *Las Posadas*.

The Jesse Tree

So much of who we are has roots in persons and events that precede us. The person of Jesus and the Christian faith is no different. We are so dependent on the foundation that Judaism and the Hebrew Scriptures provide for us. The Jesse Tree celebrates this heritage and allows us to tell the stories of those who prepared the way for Jesus.

The name for the tree comes from Scripture: "But a shoot shall sprout from the stump of Jesse, and from his roots a bud shall blossom" (Isaiah 11:1). Jesse was the father of King David from whose family Jesus came.

Each day of Advent, then, the trunk of the Jesse Tree is built up (branched) with a faith ancestor of Jesus. For example, on the first day the story (depending on the age of the group you may substitute the story with a reading from Scripture) of Adam and Eve is told followed by the hanging on the tree of a symbol (an apple) representative of them. Subsequent days follow until the end of Advent and the beginning of Christmas. By this time the Jesse Tree should be "green" with symbols and both young and old should have a good grasp of Jesus' ancestors in faith.

An interesting twist you may want to add to the Jesse Tree is to have your children or students bring a picture of someone in their family who has been important in their own family history. The mixture of classic and new would make for an interesting Jesse Tree.

The Advent Wreath

Another popular Advent symbol is the Advent Wreath. Though the origins of this symbol predate Christianity, it is synonymous with Advent today. While we often focus on the candles and their colors, the real symbol of the wreaths are the lit flames. In this way, we proclaim and prepare for the coming of the light of the world, Jesus Christ.

The wreath itself is in the shape of a circle, a symbol of God's eternity. The green color speaks of life and health. The four candles represent the four weeks of Advent. Traditionally, three of the candles are purple for the penitential character of the season. One, though, is rose (or pink) for the third week (*Gaudete* or "Rejoice" Sunday).

Whether at Mass, at home, or in the classroom, the basic ritual includes an initial blessing of the wreath followed by a weekly prayer and lighting of the candle. You could lead this or choose others to do so.

Las Posadas and Nativity scene

The season would be incomplete without a nativity or manger scene. Popularized by Saint Francis of Assisi, it lets us picture the reality of the incarnation—Jesus becoming one with us. Given the season, one should gradually put the various characters out, withholding the infant Jesus until Christmas day.

Given the increasing presence of Hispanic Catholics in the United States, I'd encourage you to consider *Las Posadas.* This is a Mexican celebration connected with Advent. The word means "inns" and reenacts Joseph and Mary's trip from Nazareth to Bethlehem and their difficulty in finding shelter.

It starts on December 16 and ends December 24. Over the nine days (symbolic of Mary's pregnancy) people travel from house to house. Having been refused by several innkeepers, the last house lets them in at which point a celebration of food, drink, and dance begins.

SYMBOLS OF THE SACRAMENTS OF INITIATION: EMBARKING ON A LIFELONG JOURNEY

At the very core of our being there is a desire for relationship, for connection, for community. As experience has taught us, these relationships do not form overnight. They require a period, or process, of initiation. For example, take the "American" community that I am a part of. Growing up I learned songs ("America the Beautiful"), looked at images (the Flag), and read documents (Declaration of Independence) about what it means to be a citizen of America. Though I am an adult now, I continue to explore and to discover more about what it means to be American.

As central as being an American is to my identity there is something even more important—being a Catholic

Christian. This too entailed an initiation process. These privileged moments of encounter with God are called the sacraments of initiation—Baptism, Confirmation, and Eucharist. Though some experience them at the same time, most "cradle" Catholics receive them over an extended period of time. Whenever they are celebrated, the sacraments of initiation invite us into the life, death, and resurrection of Jesus. This is a lifelong process of conversion that will never end.

Community

Though we take it for granted, a primary symbol of the sacraments of initiation is community. Life is radically social. As infants we were dependent on others for food, clothing, and shelter. What sustained us was a community of care. Though we may think so today, we did not rear ourselves.

Likewise, as persons being initiated into the life of Christ, we need others to support and nourish us. That is why, whenever and wherever possible, the sacraments of initiation are celebrated communally. This reminds us that Christ saves us as a people first and foremost. In a culture as individualistic as our own, with its refrain of "I did it myself," this is a hard truth to live.

A powerful image of the symbol of community celebrated in Baptism is the Litany of the Saints. As weak a model of Christ that I may be, it is reassuring to know that all the saints are called upon to help incorporate my children into the community called the Catholic Church.

Water

Another foundational symbol of the sacraments of initiation is water. It would not be an overstatement to say that we are water. Our bodies are about seventy percent water. The earth's surface is about two-thirds water. Suffice it to say that water is essential to life. But we also have been reminded lately (think of any number of natural disasters—floods and hurricanes) that water can be deadly.

In Baptism, we are plunged into the waters to die to a life of sin only to rise to new life in Christ. (This symbol is conveyed far more effectively through immersion, though most of us were baptized via a small pouring.) Scripturally, we see a strong image of this in the Israelites' crossing of the Red Sea. Fleeing a life of slavery, they cross the "baptismal" and transforming waters of the Red Sea and enter the Promised Land. Likewise, in his encounter with the woman at the well (John 4:10–15), Jesus offers her (and us) living water such that we will never thirst again.

Meals

If you want to gather people together, provide food and drink and they'll come. No initiation process is complete without a meal (at least for Catholics!). This is where the Eucharist comes in. Cleansed by the waters of Baptism and enriched by the Spirit and oils during Confirmation, the banquet is now ready to be served and enjoyed.

Unlike Thanksgiving with its one table for adults and another one for children, we now sit at the table of the Lord as equal brothers and sisters. This is surely cause for "thanksgiving," which is what Eucharist means.

As the sacraments of initiation indicate, our growth in Christ is gradual. Rather than an event, it is a lifelong process of maturity.

SYMBOLS OF THE ELECTION RITE: CELEBRATING CONVERSION

The journey of Christian discipleship is one of conversion—a turning away from sin and embracing new life in

Christ. A clear expression of that conversion is the parish catechumenate—the Rite of Christian Initiation of Adults (or RCIA). Restored after the Second Vatican Council, the catechumenate is the process whereby a person, through successive periods, becomes fully initiated into Christ.

On the Journey Together

An important part of this process is the Rite of Election (also referred to as Enrollment of Names) with its numerous symbols. The rite follows a period of faith sharing, prayer, and study on the part of the catechumen. The rite usually takes place on the first Sunday of Lent. With our "Alleluias" packed away and churches bathed in purple, the Christian community readies itself for Christ's passion and resurrection. As the catechumens intensify their preparation for initiation into the Church, we join them on their journey of faith in acts of prayer, fasting, and almsgiving.

Looking at the joy and excitement on the faces of these new candidates for admission in the Catholic Church, many "cradle Catholics" are both challenged and renewed in their faith: challenged in the sense that we must give witness ourselves to the power of Christ and his Church and in our lives; renewed in the sense that the candidates' expression of faith awakens in us the love of God and neighbor.

Readiness

During the rite, the community also hears the testimony of godparents, sponsors, and catechists who represent the larger body of Christ as to the readiness of the catechumens. This witnessing is done to declare to the community the work God has done in the lives of these catechumens to ready them for discipleship. It is at this point that the Church "elects" these persons.

As the Church was elected, or chosen by God, so now the Church, acting in God's name, enrolls the catechumens in the next stage of their journey leading to initiation at the Easter Vigil. As a sign of their enrollment, the catechumens sign their names in the Book of the Elect, which lists the names of those preparing for the sacraments of initiation.

The place of the rite is very important as well. The bishop is the ordinary minister of this rite. Therefore, it is assumed the rite takes place at the cathedral, although it can be celebrated elsewhere. The cathedral is the principal church of a diocese, the mother of all the others. It is a powerful sign of unity to have all the elect gathered in one place. The bishop, on behalf of the community, declares approval of the testimony given about the candidates and offers support to them in their desire to finish the journey of communion with Christ. The elect now enter what is called the Period of Purification and Enlightenment, during which they intensify their preparation for the reception of the sacraments.

The elects' new status in faith is symbolized in two new "names" they are given—*competentes* and *illuminatio*. The first name speaks of them as "co-petitioners" "because they are joined together in asking for and aspiring to receive the three sacraments of Christ and the gift of the Holy Spirit" (*Rite of Christian Initiation of Adults*, #124). The second name means "those who will be enlightened." Baptism brings enlightenment, which is what the elect, and we supporting them, desire.

In the Rite of Election we see the mystery of God's love for us unfold.

The Lenten Scrutinies

If Lent is anything it is a time of repentance and self-examination. Individually and communally we are called to greater awareness of the power of sin in our lives so that what is weak within us can be healed and strengthened. This is symbolically and spiritually done for the elect in the scrutinies done during the final three weeks of Lent.

Through the celebration of the scrutinies, the elect come to a greater understanding of the mystery of sin and long to be delivered from its grip and consequences. Echoing the three gospel readings—the Samaritan woman at the well, the man born blind, and Lazarus' rising from the dead—the scrutinies proclaim to us that Jesus is the living water we thirst for, the light of the world that we long to see, and the resurrection that we await in faith.

The scrutinies include a rite of exorcism whereby the elect (and the faithful gathered in the assembly) are freed from the power of sin and influence of Satan as well as strengthened in the final days for their faith journey's completion in the waters of baptism.

> **Prayer of Exorcism, Third Sunday of Lent RCIA #154**
> *God of power,*
> *you sent your Son to be our Savior.*
> *Grant that these catechumens,*
> *who, like the woman of Samaria, thirst for living water,*
> *may turn to the Lord as they hear his word*
> *and acknowledge the sins and weaknesses that weigh*
> *   them down.*
> *Protect them from vain reliance on self*
> *and defend them from the power of Satan.*
> *Free them from the spirit of deceit,*
> *so that, admitting the wrong they have done*
> *they may attain purity of heart*
> *and advance on the way to salvation.*
> *We ask this through Christ our Lord. Amen.*

SYMBOLS OF THE EASTER VIGIL: PLUNGE INTO THE PRESENCE OF GOD

For so many reasons and in so many ways, it's easy to "fall asleep." Yet, Christians are called to be a watchful, vigilant people. Nowhere is this better evidenced than at the Easter Vigil, the night of nights. On this night the Church tells the story of salvation history, which culminates in the celebration of the Resurrection of Jesus. For good reason then, Saint Augustine called it the "mother of all vigils." The four liturgical movements of the Easter Vigil—light, word, water, and meal—plunge us into the presence of God.

You are the Light of the World

We gather in darkness, seeking the light. A blazing fire, the light of the world, is ignited to break apart the darkness and gather the community in warmth.

We bless the fire, taking from it a light for the paschal candle as the presider proclaims: "May the Light of Christ, rising in glory, dispel the darkness of our hearts and minds."

We follow the paschal candle in procession to hear God's word. Along the journey, we sing: "Christ our light." "Thanks be to God." Before we hear God's word, the deacon (or cantor) sings the great Easter Proclamation (Exsultet):

> *Rejoice, heavenly powers! Sing choirs of angels!*
> *Exult, all creation around God's throne!*
> *Jesus Christ, our King, is risen!*
> *Sound the trumpet of salvation!*

Word

In the Liturgy of the Word the whole story of salvation is told. From the Old Testament we hear stories of creation, the Exodus, Isaiah and Israel's covenant with God, and exile in Babylon. From Paul we are told to "consider [our]selves dead to sin and alive to God in Christ Jesus" (Rom 6:11).

Before the gospel is proclaimed, the Alleluia, unsung since the beginning of Lent, returns announcing the joy of what is to come—the Resurrection. In a culture with deafening and deadening noise in all directions, the sung Alleluia points to the voice as a symbol of unity and harmony. The gospel, of course, invites us into the resurrection experience—the symbol of life transformed. Jesus is not dead but risen.

Water

Accompanied by the Litany of Saints, "living" symbols of the resurrected Christ, and led by the paschal candle, the candidates for baptism and the ministers go to the font. There the water is blessed. In doing so we are reminded of its central role in the mystery of salvation: the Creation, the flood of Noah, the liberation of Israel through the Red Sea, and Jesus' baptism in the Jordan. After the baptisms, the faithful are blessed with water recalling their own death to sin and rebirth in Christ.

Meal

The newly initiated are now called to the table of the Lord for the first time. Transformed through fire, word, and water, they eat what they are—the body and blood of Christ.

SYMBOLS OF THE HOLY SPIRIT: WE ARE TRANSFORMED BY GOD'S GIFTS

As Catholics we're conditioned to begin everything with, "In the name of the Father, Son, and Holy Spirit." In fact, the Church's chief liturgical expression and event, the Mass—the drama of Jesus Christ's life, death, and resurrection, begins this way. Though many of us are able to grasp and relate to both the Father and Son, the Spirit, unfortunately, remains elusive. One way we can better relate to and understand the Holy Spirit is to become aware and appreciate its symbolic presence in the liturgy.

Water and the Spirit

Some time, watch how many people cross themselves with holy water as they enter church. It reminds me of the creation story (Genesis 1:1–2). The earth was a formless wasteland with darkness covering the abyss. Into this, though, came a mighty wind—the Spirit of God—which swept over the waters.

Where there was waste, the Spirit brought forth abundant life. Where there was darkness, the Spirit brought light. Each week, through the celebration of the Mass, the Holy Spirit places before us the opportunity for recreating ourselves and the world in the image and likeness of God. In the midst of our hurried and hectic lives, we are given a foretaste of this invitation when we bless ourselves with holy water.

Color of the Spirit

The primary color of the Holy Spirit is red. We see this particularly in the liturgy. The presider wears red on the feast of Pentecost and on martyrs' feast days. Red symbolizes the tongues of fire that descended upon the apostles as they went out to preach the Gospel. Red also symbolizes blood, and so it is used to mark the power of the Spirit in the witness of the faith of those who died for the gospel.

Word, Eucharist, and Assembly

Beginning his public ministry in Nazareth, Jesus goes to the synagogue on the Sabbath and reads from a scroll of the prophet Isaiah: "The spirit of the Lord is upon me, because he has anointed me to bring glad tidings to the poor" (Luke 4:16). When we hear the word of God proclaimed, we know the Holy Spirit is present. It is a prophetic presence, which calls us to become, like Jesus, agents of justice.

This presence of the Holy Spirit, as the Word of God reminds us, has been with the Church from the beginning. We only need to recall it—Creation, Exodus, Resurrection, Pentecost—through the proclaimed word "which thus awakens the memory of the Church then inspires thanksgiving and praise (doxology)" (*Catechism of the Catholic Church*, #1103).

The greatest gift of the liturgy, though, is the Eucharist. As the Holy Spirit came upon Mary some 2,000 years ago and ushered in the Incarnation, it continues to make Jesus present to us in the Eucharist. During the Eucharistic prayer, with hands outstretched, the priest calls upon the Spirit (*epiclesis*): "Let your Spirit come upon these gifts [bread and wine] to make them holy, so that they may become for us the body and blood of our Lord, Jesus Christ" (Eucharistic Prayer II). As the bread and wine are transformed so too are we by the power of the Holy Spirit.

Another symbol of the Holy Spirit is the assembly. At first glance, however, the racial, cultural, social, economic, and political differences which we bring with us to Mass would appear to be a cause of division; an experience of Babel where tongues are confused and chaos reigns. Through the Holy Spirit, though, this diversity leads to unity where faith is awakened, hearts are converted, and the will of the Father is embraced. Pentecost is realized.

As the *Catechism* says: "The Holy Spirit's transforming power in the liturgy hastens the coming of the kingdom and the consummation of the mystery of salvation" (#1107).

QUESTIONS FOR REVIEW AND REFLECTION

- What story of Scripture is central to your life? Why?

- Discuss with one another a time in life when you had to wait for something important. What made the waiting so hard?

- When in life have you experienced another's (similar to Christ's) story of resurrection, renewal, and transformation?

ACTIVITIES

- Compare and contrast a Sunday dinner with Eucharist. Where does the word "obligation" factor into these experiences?

- Read the Sunday readings before Sunday to participate better in the upcoming liturgy.

PRAYER STARTER

Scripture is full of powerful examples of reconciliation. Read and reflect upon the story of the prodigal son (Luke 15:11–32). Spend some time in quiet reflecting upon which character in the story most resembles you.

CHAPTER 7

Symbols of the Mass

PROCESSIONS: WALKING WITH THE LORD

For the past several years, I have been able to participate in a weekend event that commemorates the deaths of six Jesuit priests, their housekeeper and her daughter, numerous women religious, and countless other unnamed men and women from Latin America.

The highlight of this trip is the solemn funeral procession that takes place Sunday morning. Gathered together with thousands of others, each of us carries a cross with the name of someone killed by political and economic injustice. As we march in procession, the victims' names are called out to which we respond: "Presente." It is a powerful and corporate expression of faith.

Journey of Discipleship

Processions are no less important and powerful during Mass—the celebration of the life, death, and resurrection of Jesus. Both functional and symbolic, the entrance procession is the first of five processions that take place during Mass. Here the priest, gathered with lectors, acolytes, and other ministers, makes his way to the altar where the drama of salvation history will unfold. Joining him symbolically, our journey of discipleship begins anew.

Although the assembly usually stands in place and only symbolically processes in, the assembly gets in on the action during Holy Week. On Palm Sunday, the faithful gather outside as they ready themselves to reenact Jesus' entry into Jerusalem. This procession of palms is recounted by Egeria in the 4th century when she visited Jerusalem during Holy Week.

During Lent, especially on Fridays, many experience a similar procession during the Stations of the Cross. As we noted earlier, the stations emerged as a substitute for those who were unable to go to the Holy Land and visit and pray at the sacred sites connected with Jesus' passion. Now, in our own parishes, groups process from one station to the next, singing and praying as they recount Jesus' last days. Some communities and parishes even have stations that take place outdoors, which only adds to the processional nature of this devotion.

Additionally, at the Easter Vigil, the assembly gathers outside at the burning fire where they receive candles. From the Paschal Candle other candles are lit that are brought into the darkness of the church showing forth the light of Christ. This also parallels the Exodus story when God led the Israelites out of slavery into freedom with pillars of fire through the waters of the Red Sea.

On special occasions we may witness the Gospel procession. Here the priest, joined by acolytes carrying candles and the censer, takes the Book of Gospels from the altar and carries it to the ambo. This is followed by an incensing of the book, which represents the heart of Jesus' teachings. The Gospel is privileged as a living encounter with Christ.

Though we may miss it due to the collection taking place at the same time, the third procession is the offertory. Bread, wine, and money—the gifts of the faithful—are brought to the sanctuary.

The communion procession is probably the most familiar and active one for Catholics. A people on the move and at prayer ready themselves to receive the body and blood of Jesus. This procession is not static, but dynamic, modeling the hoped-for change that the reception of the Eucharist will bring forth in our lives.

The Mass concludes with the recessional procession. At the words: "Go in peace to love and serve the Lord," the assembly responds, "Thanks be to God." The orientation is now to bring the spirit of the resurrected Lord to the world. With the symbol of the cross leading the way, the various ministers of the liturgy come out followed by the priest.

Just as walking is good for our physical heath, so too is processing good for our spiritual heath. It reminds us that we are a pilgrim people; a people on the move.

BODY LANGUAGE: IT'S HOW WE SAY IT

Though it's a learned art, one of the most important things someone can realize is how to interpret nonverbal communication. These nonverbal cues take place not only in the context of our personal relationships, but also are expressed liturgically at Mass in our relationship with God.

Genuflecting

Prior to the liturgical reforms of the Second Vatican Council, a frequent expression of devotion Catholics made upon entering church was genuflection, when a person lowers themselves to one knee. This was due to the placement of the tabernacle (which contains the reserved Blessed Sacrament) behind the main altar. The practice originated during the Middle Ages when a vassal would show respect and honor to the lord by genuflecting. Fittingly, this was transferred to how one should act in the presence of the Blessed Sacrament. In a sign of respect, many still genuflect today when entering and leaving a church.

In the context of the Mass the three most common bodily gestures made nowadays are standing, sitting, and kneeling. In their own way all of them express reverence and love of God in the person of Jesus Christ. When done collectively as a community, they also unite the assembly together in prayer.

Standing

When we hear the words, "Please rise," our attention level is heightened. Not only is standing a call to prayer, but a chief posture of it. It is also one that most religions share in one form or another. For Christians, however, in light of the resurrection, standing communicates a sense of joy and thanksgiving.

Sitting

Though I don't mean it to be taken this way, sometimes when I tell people to sit down, they think they can take a break and "veg out." During the first two readings of the Mass, the psalm response, and the homily sitting invites the worshiper to relax in such a way that they're attentive to the proclaimed word of God. Also, sitting is appropriate for times of prayerful meditation—before church, after communion, and after Mass. For the Gospel reading, though, the assembly is again asked to stand.

Kneeling

Kneeling is a symbol of adoration, humility, and penance. American Catholics most often associate this during Mass with the Eucharistic prayer, which celebrates the mystery of our salvation. It is proper that when we ask the Spirit through the priest celebrant to transform the bread and wine, these gifts of human hands, into the body and blood of Jesus, we do so kneeling. In our individualistic and competitive culture, kneeling is looked upon negatively, a sign of weakness. Liturgically speaking, however, it expresses that we are in the presence of, and are in need of, someone far greater than ourselves.

As the assembly sits, stands, and kneels, it should be noted that the priest may be using different gestures than we are. These may include bowing, signs of the hands, and the like. Like our own postures and gestures, they too reveal the presence of God in our midst.

It must not be forgotten that due to health limitations some people cannot perform certain liturgical gestures. When witnessing people in this situation our first response should be to give them the benefit of the doubt and look upon them as no less engaged in prayer than we are.

FEET WASHING: JESUS' MANDATUM

One of the most powerful symbols of the Mass happens only once a year. It takes place during Holy Week on *Mandatum* Thursday, which begins the Easter Triduum. On Holy Thursday the Church recalls the Last Supper—the Eucharist—when Jesus commanded his disciples to "do this in memory of me." The Church knows well and experiences on a frequent basis this symbol of sacrifice, meal, and memory.

The Gospel of John relates that, at the Last Supper, Jesus, in a supreme symbol of service, also washed the feet of his disciples: "Now that I, your Lord and Teacher, have washed your feet, you also should wash one another's feet. I have set you an example that you should do as I have done for you. I tell you the truth, no servant is greater than his master, nor is a messenger greater than the one who sent him" (John 13:14–16).

In appreciating the substance of this symbol, it is important to recall the cultural context of Jesus' day. Walking was common in the ancient world. Without the technology that we take for granted today, it was the primary means of transportation. Naturally, given the standard footwear of the day, the feet of walkers got dirty and smelly. For practical purposes, people needed to wash their feet. Most persons washed their own feet. Or a slave washed the owner's feet.

Master to Servant

At times, though, in a gesture of deep respect and humility, a disciple may have washed the master's or teacher's feet. It would have been quite unusual and contrary to the social norms of the day for the master—in this case Jesus—to wash the feet of his disciples. Yet, Jesus goes beyond the boundaries of what would have been considered hospitable in his day and performs a lesser task.

Interestingly, Peter resists at first, but then appears to try to move Jesus' action from one of service to subjugation: "Not just my feet but my hands and my head as well" (13:9). Jesus has to call him back to recognize that this is an act of sacrificial love. Amazingly, this symbol of love was so great that it didn't exclude anyone, even the disciple who was to betray Jesus.

What a challenging symbol we're invited to participate in on Holy Thursday! On this evening, following the
homily, the example of Jesus is imitated. The priest, a representative of Jesus, ritually reenacts this commandment of
Jesus. In the past, the ritual only included men, but today
women are allowed to fully participate. In some places,
adaptation has taken place to allow more people to participate in the meaning and experience of the symbol. For
example, some parishes have set up stations where parish-
ioners wash one another's hands saying: "I have come to
serve not be served."

Naturally, on this day, thought should be given as to
how concrete actions of service can follow this symbol of
selfless service.

"BE QUIET. BUT IT'S MASS!": MUSIC AS SYMBOL

Some people like to associate holiness with words like
quiet, calm, and *hushed.* Though it may surprise some,
words like *celebration, acclamation,* and *noise* should be
added to that list as well. In other words, music is a key
symbol of the Mass.

Often underestimated and even under-appreciated,
music is an essential part of our liturgical experience, part
of our human experience for that matter. It is a language in
and of itself. Music powerfully indicates the life and vital-
ity of a worshipping community. It allows people to hear
and feel what a community values, what its goals are, and,
ultimately, who its God is. We communicate so much by
our singing or, sadly, lack thereof.

As the United States Catholic Bishops' document *Music
in Catholic Worship* (MCW) makes clear: "Among the many
signs and symbols used by the Church to celebrate its

faith, music is of preeminent importance. Music should assist the assembled believers to express and share the gift of faith that is within them and to nourish and strengthen their interior commitment of faith."

In the Psalms (66:1–2), Scripture tells us to: "Shout joyfully to God, all you on earth, sing praise to the glory of God's name; proclaim his glorious praise!" Thankfully, during Mass, whether it is the Introductory, Communion, or Concluding Rite, or the Liturgy of the Word or Eucharist, there is ample opportunity.

The Second Vatican Council in the *Constitution on the Sacred Liturgy* stresses that "sacred music increases in holiness to the degree that it is intimately linked with liturgical action, winningly expresses prayerfulness, promotes solidarity, and enriches sacred rites with heightened solemnity" (#112). One of the chief ways to achieve this is through the "full, conscious and active participation" (#14) of the assembly.

Everybody Raise Your Voice

As valuable and necessary as a choir or cantor may be for liturgy, nothing can take the place of the assembly united in song praising God. In this case the choir or cantor doesn't add to or take over, but enhances and enriches the assembly's "voice." A key concern, as the recent Bishops' statement *Sing to the Lord: Music in Divine Worship* points out, is that the music be within the congregation's ability. Some parishes desire variety and are able to learn songs quickly, while for others it is better that they have a stable set of songs they know and can sing well (#27). Capability communicates effectiveness.

When selecting music that invites the community's involvement, a threefold judgment (MCW #25–41) needs to be considered. First, the musical judgment asks, "Is the music good—technically, aesthetically, and expressively?" Second, the liturgical judgment sees if the nature of the liturgy is respected. This will determine the kind of music (classic, contemporary, folk, or cultural) chosen and what parts to sing and who will sing them. Third, the pastoral judgment questions whether the music enables the people to express their faith, in this place, in this age, in this culture.

When speaking of Christ's presence in the Mass most people today realize it in the Eucharist, the proclaimed Word, the priest, and the assembly. But, as the symbol of music makes clear, Christ is present when the Church sings.

COLOR AND TIME AS SYMBOLIC

For those who like to characterize the Church as "black and white," all they need to do is participate in a liturgy and they will be convinced otherwise. Mass is, to say the least, a very colorful experience. These colors are intimately associated with the liturgical year, which sees time as sacred and a place where we experience the grace of God.

As for the color of vestments, the *General Instruction on the Roman Missal* states that: "Variety in the color of the vestments is meant to give effective, outward expression to the specific character of the mysteries of the faith being celebrated and, in the course of the year, to a sense of progress in the Christian life" (#307).

A Rainbow of Faith

Technically not a color in the truest sense of the term, white brings forth images of innocence and purity (white wedding). During Christmas and Easter, white will adorn both persons and objects used in the liturgy. It is also the color that clothes those newly initiated into the Church, who are now clothed in Christ. Prior to the reforms of the Second Vatican Council black was used at funerals. Today it has been supplanted by the color white, which emphasizes the themes of joy and resurrection.

The color red is most often associated with the season of Pentecost. This time of the liturgical year commemorates the beginning of the Church, when the Spirit descended like tongues of fire upon the Apostles and disciples of Jesus. Red also brings to mind blood and is seen on days that the Church celebrates the feasts of martyred saints. The color is also seen on Passion (Palm) Sunday and Good Friday.

Say Advent and Lent and the color purple (and violet) immediately comes to mind. In Advent we await the multiple comings of Jesus—at Christmas, in our daily lives, and still yet to come. Unlike Lent with its themes of fasting, mourning, and penance, during Advent the color purple speaks to preparation for and anticipation of the Incarnation. As a symbol of royalty, purple also images Christ the King.

Green is a color that is often associated with Christmas but is used most often during Ordinary Time. It is a color associated with life. As spring emerges from winter, green seems to be everywhere. Both naturally and symbolically, green pictures the triumph of life over death.

Two other colors bear mentioning. The first is blue. This is associated with Mary. Though the origins are unclear, it could speak to her mediating role between heaven and earth as, from her very person, Jesus—fully human and fully divine—came to reconcile God and humanity. Yellow is another color that is sometimes seen, which represents light and divinity.

THE SIGN OF THE CROSS:
A SIMPLE YET PROFOUND SYMBOL

The gift of the most powerful and moving symbols is that they can communicate so much through so little movement and words. Such is the case with the Sign of the Cross. Unfortunately, many symbols also can lose their effect due to frequent usage. The familiar often is taken for granted. Such is the case with the Sign of the Cross.

It is with this symbol, though, that the whole of Christian faith is summarized. Many enter church instinctively placing their hands in the baptismal font, after which they sign themselves in the name of the Father, of the Son, and of the Holy Spirit. If we only knew what we were communicating, I think we'd often have to stop in our tracks.

For the Sign of the Cross physically brings to bear the great mystery, the great relationship, of our faith—the Trinity. This triune, three-personed, community of love offers itself to us through the incarnation of the Son in Jesus and, later, sanctifies us with the gift of the Holy Spirit. Most explicitly, it expresses the fullness of God's love and utter vulnerability for us—Jesus' death on the cross. Through this hand movement we profess faith in the Christ we claim as savior.

So primary a symbol is this that each Mass begins with it. As we ready ourselves to celebrate the life, death, and resurrection of Jesus, we do so with the Sign of the Cross. In this sense, the Sign of the Cross gives birth to our faith for we were signed with it at our Baptisms. Before the Gospel is proclaimed we again make the Sign of the Cross. What is the Word of God proclaimed but a testament to this sign? During the Eucharistic Prayer, the priest blesses the bread and wine such that, in and through this sign, they are transformed into the Body and Blood of Christ.

Finally, prior to the assembly's dismissal, they are marked by the Sign of the Cross, which takes them out into the world to be that very sign to others.

Sanctifying Sign

If I didn't know better, I'd think a pattern of multiplication was emerging. Tertullian, an early Church Father (230 AD), makes explicit what I already know intuitively when he writes: "In all our actions, when we come in or go out, when we dress, when we wash, at our meals, before resting to sleep, we make on our forehead the Sign of the Cross. These practices are not commended to us by a formal law of Scripture, but tradition teaches them, and faith observes them."

Tertullian might cringe, however, for if he were present today he might see a basketball player make the Sign of the Cross before a free throw, a boxer before he enters the ring, a baseball player before he steps into the batter's box, or a football player after he scores a touchdown. It is no mere superstition or good luck charm.

The Sign of the Cross expresses the sum and substance of faith that we are born into, die with, and rise again with Christ Jesus. We are called to make ourselves and the world holy through it.

EUCHARIST: SACRAMENT OF THANKSGIVING

Depending on the Sunday, either my wife or I will carry our three-year old daughter up to communion. Holding her in my arms, processing forward, I can't help but be a proud daddy. It's a moment of real physical and spiritual intimacy. Invariably, though, after seeing me receive communion, Nora asks the question: "Can I have some?"

Frustratingly, my vast theological education is for naught as, at times, I try to distract her and avoid a response altogether; while at others, I say, "Not right now. You have to wait until you're as old as Cara" (her older sister).

In the Catholic tradition, we err on the side of understanding and intellect over experience. Surely, for this reason, it's impossible for a three-year-old to receive communion.

The Power of Symbols

Transubstantiation and real presence are concepts foreign to the mind of young children. Yet, we can't forget the reality and power of symbols that touch us at levels far deeper than the rational. Nor can we underestimate symbols' effect on children. My daughter sees her family eating at the altar of Lord and asks to be fed as well. For me my daughter's request is a powerful symbol of and desire for community. Will this deep experience of hers be met with acceptance or rejection?

Ultimately, that is what the Eucharist is: God inviting us to the table to participate in the supreme sacrifice of community—the death of Jesus for all of creation. This act of universal and unconditional love provides those who partake of its nourishment so they are then able to go forth and feed others. As the term *Eucharist* itself means, what an experience of "thanksgiving."

Questionable Friends

One thing that both amuses and frightens me about Jesus are his table manners or, better put, his table mates. Not only was he accused of being a glutton and drunkard (not someone you would ordinarily hang around), but his choice of companions at table—tax collectors and sinners—left a little (actually a lot) to be desired (Luke 7:34).

I spend the better part of my week trying to convince myself and others that I'm a good person. Therefore I try to spend as little time as possible with "tax collectors and sinners." Thankfully, prior to receiving communion, I am asked to voice the words: "Lord, I am not worthy to receive you, but only say the word and I shall be healed." It is here where I am forced to recognize the person—a sinner—I have been hiding from for the majority of the week. Myself. To this, Jesus' response is always, "Come, receive my body, drink my blood." His table fellowship, his love, his breaking of any number of false boundaries, is, indeed, liberating.

Now, don't get me wrong, I am not arguing to change the current Eucharistic practice of the Catholic Church. What I am saying, however, is that when it comes to understanding the fullness of the Eucharist as symbol, we're all children.

QUESTIONS FOR REVIEW AND REFLECTION

- Movement, or processions, is such a major part of our lives. Far too often, though, when we move we go with the flow, not thinking of the direction we are taking. Where have you gone lately? What physical and spiritual movements are taking place in your life? Are you headed in the right direction?

- What is communicated to ourselves and others when we make the sign of the cross? Where do you make the sign of the cross? Are there places where you won't? Why?

- How does the Eucharist feed you? In what ways does it call you to a life of greater simplicity and sacrifice?

ACTIVITIES

- Whatever hesitation you may have, make a commitment that the next time you're at Mass, you will join the community in song and praise.

- Entering into the spirit of Jesus' command to wash someone's feet, arrange a visit to a soup kitchen, homeless shelter, tutoring center, etc., where concern for justice is put into action.

PRAYER STARTER

Read Luke 24:13–35 (The Appearance of Jesus on the Road to Emmaus).

Has Jesus ever walked with you on your faith journey? Like his disciples with him on the road, have you ever struggled to believe that we are saved through a crucified Christ? How do you respond to other people's testimony (He is risen) of the role that Jesus plays in their lives? When have you discovered Jesus in the breaking of the bread?